NO WAY OUT?

BERNARD HÄRING

NO WAY OUT?

Pastoral care
of the divorced and remarried

 St Paul Publications

Original title: *Ausweglos? Zur Pastoral bei Scheidung und Wiederverheiratung. Ein Plädoyer* © Verlag Herder, Freiburg im Breisgau 1989

Translated by Robert Nowell

Cover photo: by L. Lees

St Paul Publications
Middlegreen, Slough SL3 6BT, England

English translation copyright © St Paul Publications 1990

First printed: April 1990. Reprinted: December 1990

Printed by The Guernsey Press Co., Guernsey C.I.

ISBN 0 85439 317 X

St Paul Publications is an activity of the priests and brothers of
the Society of St Paul who proclaim the Gospel through the media of
social communication

Contents

FOREWORD   9

I. WAYS OUT   13
1. "I know I am a great sinner"   13
2. "I knew this hour would come at last"   15
3. "I am a sinner. I cannot any longer stand being praised"   16
4. The impotent man with three doctorates and the incompetent canon lawyer   16
5. "I have experienced the healing Church"   17
6. "Now I am reconciled to the approach of death"   18
7. Moral insensitivity or sinful structures?   20
8. A radical new challenge to the Church   21

II. OLD AND NEW PARADIGMS:
   RETHINKING
   AND STRUCTURAL REFORMS   27
1. Law and grace or grace and law?   27
2. The decisive role of our understanding of the sacraments.   32
3. Examination of the anthropological foundations   36

III. THE HOPED-FOR NEW VISION –
   THE SPIRITUALITY
   AND PRACTICE OF ECONOMY   39
1. What does the spirituality of economy mean?   40

2. The application of economy to the doctrine of
   the indissolubility of marriage 41
   (a) "Till death do us part" 43
   (b) The "moral death" of a marriage 44
   (c) The "psychic death" of the spouse 46
   (d) "Civil death" 48
3. The blessing of a second marriage in the form
   influenced by economy 49

IV. HOW IN OUR CHURCH CAN WE REACH
    A PRACTICE BASED ON THE PRINCIPLE
    OIKONOMIA 53
1. The superiority of a spirituality based on the
   principle of *oikonomia* 53
2. Psychotherapy in the spirit of the spirituality
   of economy 55

V. FIRST STEPS TOWARDS A REFORM OF
   THE LAW 59
1. Overcoming a harsh tutiorism in the Church's
   nullity procedure 59
2. Respecting the basic human right to marriage 61
3. On whom does the burden of proof fall? 62

VI. WHAT CAN BE DONE TODAY IN
    ADVANCE OF ANY REFORM OF THE LAW? 65
1. Relapse into legalism or pressing forward at
   the wrong time? 65
2. What in any case we should do or refrain from
   doing 66
3. Psychotherapeutic efforts at reconciliation 68
4. To what extent should we encourage recourse to
   epikeia and to what extent should we tolerate it? 70

5. *Epikeia* with regard to the practice of annulment   73
6. Solutions in the internal forum   75
7. How high must the requirements for
    absolution be?   78
8. Reconciliation after the breaking up of a marriage
    brought about by disgraceful behaviour   82

IN CONCLUSION   87

NOTES   89

Foreword

Faced with the increasing number of divorces and the intolerable suffering of those involved, the Church is called upon to show its wisdom and its true visage. Will it always understand more deeply that it is being called by the master who said of himself: "I did not come to judge the world but to save the world" (Jn 12:47)? Will it be able to free itself from depending on the letter in favour of complete loyalty towards its divine founder whose basic law runs: "Be merciful, even as your Father is merciful" (Lk 6:36)? From the treasure of revelation and its various traditions will it find ways that will enable marriage to be better understood and grasped as a vocation to free faithfulness while also taking into consideration things as they are here and now, and this in such a way that its doctrine and attitude demonstrate unwavering loyalty towards the master who teaches us by word and example that the sabbath and every law is made for man and not man for the law? What is involved is the vocation of the entire Church and of all Christians to exemplary fidelity and to peace. What is primarily and ultimately involved is whether the Church in its entire existence, in its dealing with the law of Christ and in its turning to those who have been hurt or who have failed, can ever more strongly be experienced as the sacrament of Christ's reconciling mercy.

This is something that challenges all of us. The present situation challenges me as someone who has retired after fifty years' activity as a moral theologian and as a priest dealing with people to utter what is perhaps my last word of encouragement, out of sympathy not only with those who are divorced but also with the bishops and all who are active in pastoral work. Perhaps this word of encouragement and sympathy belongs to my immediate preparation for death, in confident reliance on the Lord's promise: "Blessed are the merciful, for they shall obtain mercy" (Mt 5:7).

I am aware of the passionate search for a solution, a search moulded by suffering, on the part of many bishops, priests and pastorally active lay people. What will the Redeemer say to us with regard to this new class of excluded lepers to whom he would like to say through us: "Take courage"?

I felt encouraged when at the 1980 Synod of Bishops on the family the bishops decided on a statement that fully corresponds to my intention and when the Pope included it in his apostolic exhortation *Familiaris consortio* (§84): "Pastors must know that, for the sake of truth, they are obliged to exercise careful discernment of situations. There is in fact a difference between those who have sincerely tried to save their first marriage and have been unjustly abandoned, and those who through their own grave fault have destroyed a canonically valid marriage. Finally, there are those who have entered into a second union for the sake of the children's upbringing, and who are sometimes subjectively certain in conscience that their previous and irreparably destroyed marriage had never been valid." The Pope goes on fully to accept the bishops' concern: "Together with the Synod, I earnestly call upon pastors and the whole community of the faithful to help the [remarried] divorced, and with solicitous care to make sure that they do not consider themselves as separated from the Church." It is also recognized that, "for serious reasons, such as for example the children's upbringing, a man and a woman cannot satisfy the obligation to separate".

What was even more encouraging was that the proposal put forward by a great friend of mine among the synod fathers – that serious examination should be made of whether the Roman Catholic Church could not learn and accept something from the *oikonomia* of the Eastern Churches – was endorsed by over 90 per cent of the votes. We are on the way towards a more careful cultivation of the gift of discernment and towards a healing approach to this difficult problem.

We are on the way, but we would like gratefully to acknowledge that not only theologians but also the pastors of the Church in their overwhelming majority are on the way, as a pilgrim Church, towards ever greater fidelity to the all-merciful God, towards our redeemer Jesus Christ.

1

Ways out

I would like to use six instances which have stamped themselves on my memory to introduce some of these divorced brothers and sisters of ours. They are people like us, they have suffered more than us, and they outdo us in strength of belief, staying power, suffering and love for a Church that often seems not to understand them.

1. *"I know I am a great sinner"*

While I was a visiting lecturer in the United States I helped out in a parish with consultations for people bothered by serious problems. A man of Irish extraction told me his story, which would have been worth recording in a film. "Father, I know I am a great sinner," he said. "But I think you will understand me." Seventeen years ago he had married a pretty girl. He knew she had had an affair with another man before, but she promised him faithfully that this was all over. Within the year she presented him with a lovely baby, "flesh of his flesh". The next year a baby boy was born, the fruit of adultery with her former lover. The third child was perhaps his, but he wasn't sure. Then two more followed who were certainly the other man's. Finally his wife went off with her lover and left him with the five children, the youngest only six weeks old. "I promised Jesus that I would be a good father to all five, because after all he loves them all." The man, a simple worker, needed a mother for "his" five children. He summed things up in a typically Irish way: "A Church annulment did not come into question: it would work to the detriment not only of the mother of the five children but also to the dishonour of the children themselves. To do that to them would be a great sin. God will forgive me the sin of a second, civil marriage. But I do not want to lead anyone else into sin." So he married a single woman who had never been baptized. She was, he told me with tears in his eyes, the best imaginable mother for the five children, and presented him with two more of their own. "But now," he concluded his story, "I can no longer cope with seeing myself excluded from the sacraments. None of the priests I have spoken to wanted to give me absolution." The longer I spoke to him the more I looked up to him, full of respect. I didn't tell him that. But he went home comforted and started taking part fully in the sacramental life of the Church again. Within the year he came back to see me with his wife, who has signed up for instruction with a view to baptism. The reason was the joy that her husband was now deriving from his faith. She, however, wanted her husband to take part in the instruction too, because she thought his religious convictions were a little too narrow in some things. In nearly everything I was able to agree that the wife was right, and her husband was happy with this. He gladly liberated himself to accept a more mature faith. The parish priest of this parish joined in rejoicing over the moving ceremony of baptism and confirmation.

The day I had proposed was the exact anniversary of their civil wedding. No one thought of a wedding, which would all the same have been conceivable on the grounds of *epikeia* or equity (cf. pp. 70 ff.). Everyone was con-

14

vinced that God had already richly blessed this marriage. Not even canon law had to be infringed.

2. *"I knew this hour would come at last"*

After a lecture for honorary teachers of religion in the USA, a twenty-year-old teacher of religion asked me for an appointment for an extensive talk with his father who, according to his son, was close to a mental breakdown. His excellent wife had died after the birth of their seventh son. Nobody wanted to act as housekeeper for seven small boys. An Anglican woman who had been deserted by her husband took pity on them. She was the best mother imaginable for the seven boys, as both the young man and his father told me. The Sunday after their civil wedding the parish priest, in the middle of the sermon, pointed at this widely respected man and said: "Look at someone who wants to go to hell!" His Anglican wife was not able to get her previous marriage declared null because her ex-husband refused to testify. The family prayed a great deal. The Anglican wife accompanied her husband and the children to Mass every Sunday. But the husband felt he was excluded from receiving the sacraments. I gave him absolution without any hesitation: a "saint" who even got sympathy from the parish priest who slung him out of his church. *Epikeia* was clearly called for here. With tears in his eyes the man said to me: "I knew somehow or other that this hour would come at last." The family was then living in a town where nobody knew about the "invalidity" of their marriage. No subsequent marriage ceremony took place. Was this couple not already, through God's grace, a sign of the healing power of love and its ability to make people happy?

3. *"I am a sinner. I cannot any longer stand being praised"*

For years a Catholic man kept up a correspondence with me. He also travelled a long way to see me and to discuss his case with me in person. When he returned home from London after taking the examination for his doctorate his wife had gone off with another man. All his efforts and those of his friends did not succeed in persuading the wife to return to her husband. A nullity decree turned out to be impossible. For fifteen years this devout believer remained unmarried. He was even held up in public as an example by bishops because he went on living singly in loyalty to the Church's teaching and law. He wept as he told me: "And yet I am a great sinner. Hardly a year has not passed when I have not sinned with a woman and shared in responsibility for her sin." Finally he wrote to me that he had now decided to enter a second marriage even though it was impossible for this to be recognized by the Church. He was doing this not only because he felt desperately lonely but also and above all because he was quite simply no longer able to see himself held up as an example when in reality he was anything but. I was extremely sad when I had read his letter, and I found it very difficult to answer. But I did not skip this pastoral duty. I leave it to the reader to work out what I wrote to this man after he or she has read through the whole of this book.

4. *The impotent man with three doctorates and the incompetent canon lawyer*

A sensitive, well-educated Italian woman told me her story. She had then been waiting three years for a statement on her nullity plea to a Church marriage tribunal. Her husband had three doctorates and was a total slave to his career. This may perhaps also explain his sexual impotence. He was incapable of consummating the marriage, and at the same time incapable of showing affection to his wife. She stuck it out for five years in the hope of being able to "cure" him: in vain. She obtained a civil divorce without any difficulty. The Church marriage tribunal, however, demanded three times in the course of the three years an examination to see if her hymen was intact. Each time the result was the same: it was. When the third examination in three years was asked for, her father wanted to leave the Church in protest. She was eventually able to dissuade him by talking to him affectionately. Her argument was: "These poor petty-minded lawyers aren't the Church. They are the sad result of the wrong kind of education and deserve our pity." She got married at last when her nullity decree came through – after four years of waiting. I could only boggle at her composure and patience. I am not surprised if many others are simply not capable of this kind of patience and this kind of generous forgiveness.

5. *"I have experienced the healing Church"*

Catholic nuns looked me up in New York to talk to a young black woman from Harlem. She had been a complete drug addict, the mother of a delightful little girl, and the nuns had taken her into their house and cured her both physically and mentally. The young woman now wanted to get married. When she was sixteen she had let herself be forced by her mother into a Catholic marriage because she was pregnant. The father of her child was an immature eighteen-year-old. During the first week of their marriage he went for his wife with a kitchen knife and wounded her.

After six weeks she escaped with severe stab wounds and in a severe state of shock. Even after she had been cured she did not dare visit that part of town again. Now she had a boyfriend whom the nuns, who had looked after her so affectionately, considered good and mature. The diocesan marriage tribunal responded to her plea for her first marriage to be declared null by saying nullity was "unprovable" since her ex-husband could not be found. Living as a single parent in the big city seemed quite simply unreasonable not just to her but also to the nuns. But the young woman did not want to do anything that she understood as rebellion against the Church. She said: "I love my Church now, since with the nuns I have experienced the love of the Church." The good nuns found a solution. They went to a parish priest who dealt with the matter according to *epikeia*, particularly because one of the canon lawyers on the tribunal let him know that the nullity decree had failed because of the resistance of a far-too-legalistic-minded priest. How many women in similar situations have not had the good fortune to meet nuns with such motherly hearts and concerns!

6. *"Now I am reconciled to the approach of death"*

A friend of mine who had lost his larynx, a belated emigrant from Poland, was struck down with cancer just when he had re-established himself in his new homeland. The similarity of our diseases led to a friendship that meant a great deal for his whole family. On one visit he and his wife told me about the marriage of his wife's sister, who like them was now in Germany with her husband. Briefly, the story was that this devout Catholic found soon after her Catholic wedding that for the sake of his career her husband had joined the Communist Party and wanted her too to stop going to church. At the same time he didn't want to have any children. They obtained a civil divorce, and she was convinced that the Church would declare her marriage null. But this was not to be. Her divorced husband refused to testify. The judges on the marriage tribunal continued to harbour doubts. Their conclusion was that, because the case had not been cleared up one hundred per cent, the marriage could not be declared null. In a civil ceremony she married a widower who needed a mother for his young children. The fact that they could only have a civil ceremony was extremely painful for both of them. With complete loyalty they went to Mass every Sunday, said prayers at home, and in the first years of their marriage spent their time trying to find a priest who would admit them to the sacraments. In vain. Thirty years had gone by like this when, at the wish of my larynx-less friend who was close to death, I visited the family to celebrate a house Mass and to give him the sacrament of the sick. The couple, whose suffering weighed so heavily on the dying man's heart, had a long talk with me and came to confession: wonderful people, without any bitterness. Together with the dying man and his family they received communion, and they went home comforted. My friend, who was racked by terrible pain, said to me: "Now I am reconciled to the approach of death. I am so glad about those two good people. The way they were treated by the Church has often made me very sad."

Just from my own experiences I could fill a book on this subject, quite apart from the even more numerous cases told me by priest friends or by the friends of those affected. Up until about twenty years ago so many marriage tribunals were characterized by a cold and bureaucratic atmosphere which was directly opposed to the Gospel. People who have already been deeply hurt by divorce had their wounds rubbed even rawer by legal hard-heartedness.

19

People who were severely affected were left to wait for months and years, and futile demands were continually being made for new documents and witnesses. Finally the response came: "The nullity of the marriage has not been established." Even when one had to deal with canon lawyers who were humanly sympathetic there still remained the almost incredible fact that one hundred per cent certain proofs and complete documentation were "needed". If even a fraction were lacking of the certainty that had to have all-round documentation, then the legal prescription was lifelong celibacy.

7. Moral insensitivity or sinful structures?

Rigorism and bureaucratic coldness in almost all marriage questions – mixed marriages, birth control, and especially with regard to divorced people who had remarried – have over the years become a major cause of people becoming alienated from the Church and of people leaving it. An Episcopalian (Anglican) parish in Chicago confirmed more than thirty years ago that it owed more than half of its parishioners to this pattern of behaviour on the part of the Roman Catholic Church.

Should one suspect immorality here, or ought one to talk of sinful structures? Or does what Max Weber asserted at the beginning of the century apply, that Catholic priests just like bank officials are representatives of a bureaucratic culture? Were the Church authorities lacking in a readiness to learn, and if so why? Perhaps because nobody dared protest publicly. Was this the revenge for the way in which from time to time the highest church circles blocked the free development of public opinion within the Church and extinguished protest like a smouldering wick?

In numerous dioceses, especially in the English-speaking world, much has changed for the better. The procedure has been simplified and speeded up, and there is wide evidence of human sensitivity and pastoral concern.[1] One could and can, to a considerable extent, dare say to priests and to those concerned: "Take courage."

But the new Code of Canon Law has reversed significant alleviations that had been granted to individual regions. Insistence on a second hearing still continues to delay many cases. The whole system of marriage tribunals still enjoys a bad reputation to a considerable extent, perhaps in part unjustly. The tribunals are overburdened. If everyone who had good grounds for doubting the validity of a first marriage that has broken down were to apply to the Church's marriage tribunals, the whole system would seize up completely and come to a full stop. The great danger for the Church's marriage tribunals is of turning into courts of law where the healing love of the Redeemer can only with difficulty gain admission and where the Church's servants charged with a ministry of healing cannot, despite all their good will, find the atmosphere that would be favourable for the work of helping and healing.

8. *A radical new challenge to the Church*

The Church must consider seriously whether there could not be quite different methods, a quite different way of thought, and quite different institutions which would make the Church capable of being convincingly recognized and experienced by the world as the sacrament of salvation, of Christ's healing and reconciling love.

Since the Second Vatican Council the Church has been going through a phase of a new departure, an epoch-making farewell to a culture of almost total control, of legal sanctions. A new wind has been blowing, even if

21

many have been concerned to shut once again and bolt the windows that Pope John XXIII opened to let some fresh air in. But on the whole I stand by my cry of encouragement: "Take courage." We want to have the courage to look the new situation bravely in the face, soberly but also trusting in the Lord of history.

The shape and the functions of marriage and the family and their socio-economic and cultural environment have changed fundamentally. The extended family in which the unmarried, the deserted, the widowed, earlier found a home and a support no longer exists. In the industrial conurbations there is not even any neighbourly support any more. In the peasant and artisan world up to the last century it was relatively easy to come to terms with not marrying. There was no fundamental possibility of increasing the number of small peasant farms or small craft businesses. Since the beginning of the modern age there were alternatives alongside emigration: staying on as a respected uncle or aunt on the parental estate or with a married brother or sister, or by choosing the vocation to the religious life even rising one step up the social ladder.

Today the right to found one's own family, the right to marry, counts as one of the basic rights that is most strongly felt. Hence if someone whose first marriage has collapsed is prescribed celibacy, even if humanly speaking one has to admit that the failed marriage often did not stand any real chance from the start, this hurts and amazes those affected and their relatives in a way that just would not have been thinkable previously. The person on his or her own is extraordinarily vulnerable today in our industrial society with its anonymity and its erosion of order and structure. The woman who is divorced or deserted is looked on askance as a potential rival. With the collapse of the marriage every support seems to have collapsed too. The *vae soli* – "it is not good that man should be alone" – is experienced in a quite new way. Statistics show that divorced people who remain alone are more susceptible to psychosomatic illnesses than their contemporaries in the security of a family. Their suicide rate is significantly higher than that of people in sound marriages. The danger of drug addiction or alcoholism or both is worrying.[2]

Marriage today is much more vulnerable and much less protected than it was in the peasant and artisan cultures of our grandparents. People look to private life to balance the collective world of work. Very much more is expected of one's spouse, and to a considerable extent those getting married are marked by an extraordinary poverty of relationships, thanks to our consumer society and a system of public "education" directed entirely to achievement. If they do not break down, marriages last roughly twice as long as two or three generations ago: people are living longer. and today's nuclear family has lost very many functions that previously strengthened its external coherence. When the children grow up and leave home their still relatively young parents face quite new problems of how they should fill the gap that has now arisen. It is bad if they are not held together by shared ideals and a shared commitment to values and goals.

The list of changes could be continued even further. Has the Church made enough effort to link the commandment of the lofty aim of fidelity to an education for the freedom to which Christ has called us? This and many other questions arise with regard to the practical treatment of marriage and divorce and the shaping of doctrine on this issue. The institution of the Church's marriage tribunals – itself often diseased and causing disease – is only one of the symptons of a lack of adaptation.

The doctrine that has prevailed since the time of Pope Alexander III in the twelfth century – that a second marriage after the collapse of a first is as such to be condemned, unless absolute certainty exists about the invalidity of the first marriage – functioned well by and large in the culture of that time. The State protected marriage with its sanctions. The entire law of property easily pushed any idea of divorce to one side. And as we have already said, but it needs to be emphasized yet again, the separated man or woman had his or her security in the extended family. The unfortunate inability to start one's own family again was something that was shared with very many other people. It was only modern industrial society that made it economically possible for everyone to start a family.

All this and much else must be considered if the large number of those who are separated and divorced are to find themselves completely at home in the Church, especially when they feel themselves under pressure to marry again.

Decades ago I was being told by bishops, priests and lay people in Africa, in many regions of Latin America, and particularly in the Caribbean that a very large proportion of Catholics "lived together" for a long time before they were able to decide on a church wedding. The chief motive was again and again the following: "We want to die at peace with the Church and to receive the sacraments at the end. It is easier for us to come into conflict with the law of the Church for years now rather than to be excluded from the sacraments for the whole of the rest of our lives after a marriage that has broken down."

Today we are faced with the same phenomenon in our countries: marriage without a marriage certificate. It has of course a multiplicity of reasons. But very often I have heard arguments similar to those I heard earlier in Africa, in Latin America and in the Caribbean.

Even many parents who are loyal to the Church today approve of their grown-up children "living together" in a relationship similar to marriage with the same argument: "You ought not to be excluded from the sacraments for the

24

whole of the rest of your life if this first relationship breaks down." And of course this kind of marriage without a marriage certificate then breaks down even more easily.

I want to tell the reader here and now that my view is that the Catholic Church could learn a great deal from its own diverse tradition and particularly from the Eastern Churches' tradition of *oikonomia* or economy of salvation. We shall ask ourselves what exactly this means. In any case we cannot avoid a fundamental re-consideration. The disease is serious and its roots go deep. The lack of adaptation to new opportunities and new needs demands the courage for a new process of learning, open and open-ended discussion, new emphases and horizons in the entire field of education and preaching.

2

Old and new paradigms:
rethinking and structural reform

1. *Law and grace or grace and law?*

"For the law was given through Moses; grace and truth came through Jesus Christ" (Jn 1:17). Christ, as the bringer of grace, as he who through the Holy Spirit makes things possible, wants the indissolubility of marriage. If all the Jews had seen the law of the covenant from the point of view of consolation, from the point of view of Yahweh's liberating and gift-bestowing activity, Moses would not have been so powerless in the face of their hard-heartedness. Mere legalism strengthens hard-heartedness. Indissoluble fidelity thrives through acceptance of the lordship of grace: it is a sign of the coming and accepted kingdom of grace and peace.

In order to gain access to the demand for indissolubility, man must courageously enter into the sphere of redemption, through faith and in absolute openness to grace. Faith itself is the grateful, joyful reception of the rule of grace that is revealed in Christ. In Jesus's high-priestly prayer before his departure, before his total giving of himself for the salvation of the world, his disciples are completely included in the mutual love that is exchanged between the Father and the Son in the eternal primal event of giving: in the Holy Spirit. Six times the fundamental harmony of grace is touched on: "Thine they were, and thou gavest them to me" (Jn 17:6). But just as important and even more fundamental is the experience of faith that the Father has sent and given us his Son, Jesus Christ.

When we talk of indissoluble sacramental marriage it belongs above all to this encircling realm of grace. In a marriage which corresponds to the Father's plan of salvation and to the coming of Christ the spouses see each other as Theodore (the gift of God) and Dorothea (God's gift) with reference to Christ and the Church: Christ as the Father's primal gift, and the church (the disciples as a group and every true believer) as the Father's gift to Christ.

A morality of marriage which places every act of intercourse under the pressure to achieve an association that is quite one-sidedly orientated (if not perverted) to the aim of procreation does not pay sufficient account to the realm of grace, of gift-bestowing love that "bears fruit in love". The Second Vatican Council brings a liberating touch when it talks of the spouses' mutual surrender to each other and of their making each other happy by giving themselves to each other in sexual intercourse as "signs of the friendship distinctive of marriage" within the total framework of a life lived for and with each other: "This love the Lord has judged worthy of special gifts, healing, perfecting and exalting gifts of grace and of charity... The actions within marriage by which the couple are united intimately and chastely are noble and worthy ones. Expressed in a manner which is truly human, these actions signify and promote that mutual self-giving by which spouses enrich each other with a joyful and a thankful will" (*Gaudium et spes* §49).

In contrast to the Augustinian model of marriage that prevailed at that time Alphonsus Liguori wrote that there are only two essential purposes of marriage that are indispensably proper to every marriage and every married union: "mutual self-giving and the indissoluble bond". The mutual giving of oneself to each other in marriage and in sexual intercourse is aimed at strengthening and maintening the "indissoluble bond". Alphonsus does admittedly mention procreation and the relieving of the sexual urge as purposes of marriage and sexual intercourse that belong to its inner nature, but for him they are incidental. "It is certain that by excluding the innate incidental purposes, one might in some cases not only validly but also licitly contract the marriage." And Alphonsus says explicitly that what applies to marriage as such also applies to sexual intercourse.[3]

This view has absolutely nothing to do with hostility to children. It is precisely the persistent vision and fundamental decision in favour of mutual self-giving, and the strengthening of the indissoluble bond that flows from this, that is the fertile soil for truly human fruitfulness in love and for the grateful acceptance of the child that is responsibly called into existence as God's most precious gift. This belongs essentially to a morality of grace, without which talk of indissolubility would refer more to Moses than to Christ, through whom come grace and truth.

A one-sided and rigoristic narrowing down of the purposes of marriage and sexual intercourse to procreation and an incredible undervaluing of mutual self-giving even in the perspective of the indissoluble bond have unfortunately contributed to many marriages being eaten away or even undermined. To this is added an untenable identification of chastity and continence in sexual morality. It is not abstaining from the tenderness of complete self-giving in marriage but precisely tender mutual self-giving that is the core and glory of married chastity. It is only on this basis that periodic continence can be meaningfully understood and motivated.

This view of grace is not something to be tacked on externally to the doctrine of marriage: it provides its foundation. It elevates it to the sphere in which and for which Jesus said what he did about the indissolubility of marriage.

What I am trying to say here fits exactly with something Cardinal Joseph Ratzinger has said: "Instead of entering into the casuistry of interpreting the law and adopting this position or that, Jesus goes back behind law and interpretation to its origin, to what man really is and should be all about in the sight of God... Because Jesus goes back behind the level of law to the origin, his saying should not itself be seen immediately and without further ado as law: it cannot be detached from the sphere of faith and discipleship and can only have meaning in the context of the new situation opened up by Jesus and accepted in faith."[4]

As far as I can see, there is today hardly a single reputable Catholic, Orthodox or Protestant exegete who would contradict that. From it conclusions are to be drawn for fundamental pastoral consequences in loyalty to the primacy of grace over law: "You are not under law but under grace" (Rm 6:14). Legal rigorism blocks access to grace and the task of indissoluble fidelity in marriage. The whole of moral theology, the whole of preaching and pastoral work must bear witness to the fact that in Jesus has come the saving, healing truth and the kingdom of redeeming grace that sets one free and makes one loyal. We must continually be coming back to this foundation.

Here there is only one comment to be made, to begin with in the form of a question. Is the practice of marriage tribunals in agreement with this if when enquiring into the validity of the first sacramental marriage it is not concerned whether there existed at least a minimum of orientation in the faith and trust in grace and a vision of marriage as both gift and task? Is not the practice of the past and in part still of today simply falling back on an intensified vision of the law that used to be believed in the past? Do we not, through a legalistic morality and a false trust in legal sanctions, share in responsibility for the fact that to a considerable extent faith and grace do not come to fruition?

The typical Christian preaching of morality and education in the faith, however, should take the form of paraclesis, that encouragement offered in trust in the working of the Holy Spirit, to live according to the "law of grace". It is in the consistent orientation of this kind that the decisive turning-point is probably to be found. Nevertheless it is not in any way easy, since far too many Christians at all levels still have more trust in insistence on the law.

There is one misunderstanding in particular I would like to guard against. It is absolutely too little if one says that indissoluble marriage is according to the Bible an ideal, and even worse if one says it is merely an ideal. What is involved is not an ideal without any binding force but a commandment obliging the Christian fully and utterly to pursue a goal, just like loving one's enemies or the saying of Jesus: "Be merciful, even as your Father is merciful" (Lk 6:36).

This kind of commandment indicates a direction, but also obliges one to commit oneself, to prepare oneself, to train oneself to reach the goal and to practise and love the corresponding modes of behaviour. Above all what belongs to it is complete readiness both to seek and to impart healing forgiveness, as well as the practice of gratitude, of a thankful remembrance, of healing freedom from force, and prayer for loyal and understanding love.

What I regard as quite especially important is reflection on God's prevenient love and grace. If I have begun to displease God and to give way to sin, then there would be no hope of avoiding a descent down the slippery slope if God did not come to my aid with his love that anticipates our needs. He always takes the first step as far as the sinner is concerned. If we are filled with grateful amazement at this anticipatory love we are driven from within, in fact through grace, to emulate God in gratitude and to act similarly with regard to our neighbour. This applies above all as a fundamental law in marriage, with regard to the way it is by its inner nature directed towards indissoluble fidelity.

What has been said about marriage under the heading of the precept of indissolubility will only come to fruition if in the whole of moral theology and pastoral education in morality these precepts – commandments that set a goal – are given sufficient prominence. One-sided and exaggerated emphasis on commandments that fix a limit – prohibitions – as well as even demanding the fulfilment of this latter class of commandment without providing good reasons means falling back into the rule of law, which discourages people, disheartens them, or provokes them into rebellion. These commandments that set limits are salutary and helpful if they are seen fully in the perspective of the commandments that set a goal and the dominance of God's grace.

2. The decisive role of our understanding of the sacraments

Quite decisive for the pastoral care of marriage and for the Church's practice is the correct sacramental view of the order of salvation. A wrong or one-sidedly ritualistic understanding of the concept of sacrament obstructs many energies and sometimes makes sensible solutions impossible. Hence I shall offer here a sketch of an approach to the understanding of the sacraments with reference to the Church's sacramental action with regard to married people and the sacramental understanding of Christian marriage.

The primal foundation and image of sacramentality is

32

Christ. In him God's sanctifying and healing love has become completely visible and capable of being experienced. With regard to the Church and its sacramental life the decisive question is the transparence of Christ's original and primal sacramentality, in keeping with a well-known saying of Pope Leo the Great: *"Quod itaque Redemptoris nostri conspicuum fuit, in sacramenta transivit* – what became visible of our Redeemer was turned into the sacraments".[5] The Church shares in Christ's all-embracing sacramentality to the extent that it makes Christ and his gospel visible in its life and helps the faithful as a community and as individuals to become credible and effective signs of the kingdom of God's grace and love that has broken in on us in Christ. Augustine put this magnificently when he said: "What is it that is hidden and not public in the Church? The sacrament of Baptism, the sacrament of the Eucharist. For even the pagans see our good works, but the sacraments are hidden from them; but from the things they do not see arise the things they do see; just as from the depth of the cross that is fixed in the earth arises the whole cross that appears and is seen."[6]

Hence the Church must at all levels and in its whole presentation of itself, especially in its sacramental practice, though not exclusively in that, always ask itself afresh whether it is ordering, living and doing everything in such a way that it points faithfully to our Redeemer and his love for mankind. In the case of every effort to fulfil individual directions by its Divine Master it must ask itself first and last whether it is thereby providing as faithful a representation as possible of the all-merciful, healing Redeemer who brings salvation.

Above and beyond the question of the validity of the contracting of a sacramental marriage that has pushed itself into the foreground since the Council of Trent is the question of how the Church helps the believing Christian to be and to become an ever better effective sign of Christ's saving and healing love for spouse and children and milieu. Liturgical celebration and even the practice of the law are at the service of the vocation to become signs of salvation for and among each other.

A certain sacramentality can attach to all marriages of all ages, regions and religions if marriage and family and each spouse are linked to the primal source of salvation, explicitly or implicitly through fidelity and love that are true to human existence, by means of loyal, tender, caring, forgiving, reconciling, healing love. What is specifically Christian is the explicitness of faith and understanding of the faith "in Christ, through Christ, and with Christ". To become a sacrament of faith marriage needs explicit faith and the vision of faith, or at least a basic attitude and basic pattern of behaviour that correspond to the structure and dynamic of faith. This is shown above all in the basic experience of gratuitousness, thanks to which the spouses receive each other as a gift from God and grow together in gratitude and thankful love.

If this view is theologically correct – and along with the Eastern Churches I do not have any doubts about it – it must be made fruitful in the whole of pastoral care, above all in the pastoral care of marriage and in the assessment of marriages that have failed. If Christian married couples were aware of this sacramental dignity and vocation of theirs, they would overcome many obstacles relatively easily and intact and would help each other to heal wounds.

One of the profoundest differences and focuses of conflict between the Orthodox Churches as a whole and the Church of Rome has for centuries been the sacramental view of the sacrament of Penance. For the uninterrupted tradition of the Eastern Churches what is involved above all in confession in the normal run of things is praise of God's *healing* mercy and flowing from this the sacra-

34

ment's healing and saving power, while in the West it is the *judicial* function of the confessor that has for the most part pushed its way into the foreground, with all the anxiety-arousing questions about the differences that determine which category a sin falls into, the boundary between mortal and venial sins, etc. Over two hundred and fifty years ago St Alphonsus had already decided in favour of the more therapeutic view of the Eastern Churches and of one part of our Western tradition.

Today a healthy re-thinking with regard to all this is in the offing in the Catholic Church, something that can only be to the benefit of the whole Church, ecumenical concerns, and the pastoral care of marriage.

In the entire sacramental vision of the Eastern Churches, a vision to which Leo the Great still bears witness in the West, it is simply unthinkable to say to people who are fundamentally believers when they are in a difficult situation that God certainly accepts their good will and forgives them but that the way of the sacraments must remain barred to them because "objectively" they are living in a state of serious sin.[7]

In numerous conversations in Africa and with African bishops and priests I have heard time and time again how devout catechumens who before their conversion entered into a polygamy that is completely socially acceptable, react when they are told: "God certainly accepts your conversion with favour and he loves you, but you're no good when it comes to admission to the sacraments.' They can only shake their heads over the way they are told "Yes" and categorically "No" at one and the same time. For them the symbolic language of the sacraments is what is utterly decisive. Ought it not to be the same for us in Europe?

The practice of economy by the Orthodox Churches (and in part by the Eastern Churches in communion with Rome) – something we shall discuss in more detail later – has its deepest roots in their vision of the sacraments, which I have tried to describe briefly above.

3. *Examination of the anthropological foundations*

The profound differences between the practice of the Orthodox Churches and that of the Church of Rome and the West also have cultural roots and are connected with the anthropological understanding prevailing at the time of the relationship between man and woman and in particular of marriage and the Church's duties with regard to these. The strong emphasis on the juridical and judicial aspects of confession and penance in the West would not be conceivable without the Church having become inextricably intertwined with the total social and political situation (partly but not solely as a result of the papal states). Fundamental studies of the sociology of culture, religion and the family demand a thorough consideration of the value or otherwise of past models of inculturation and their eventual retention in quite different microsociological and macrosociological contexts.

In the Roman Catholic Church everything to do with sexuality does, of course, have a great deal to do with the will that undoubtedly exists to be faithful to what the Lord commanded. But it also has a great deal to do with Augustinian stringency and other similar influences.

It is simply neither possible nor sensible to want to hang on to certain formulations of norms right down to a precise form of words if one has observed the extent to which they are conditioned by interpretations of "nature", of the structure and aims of human sexuality, of the role of women, etc., that today have had fresh light thrown upon them. In the Protestant Churches (with the exception of fundamentalist groups) a great deal of reconsideration has taken place in this regard in an atmosphere of openness and honesty. In the Catholic Church the formation of public opinion could for a long time hardly make any progress at all. Well before the Second Vatican Council the situation was tense. Today, as Karl Rahner warned several years ago, the temperature has dropped back to zero again, and this makes it difficult to cooperate in investigating things and making distinctions. But if we look at the dynamics of our Church as a whole we can and should still say: "Take courage."

Throughout contemporary ecumenical theology there is apparent a deepened new understanding resting on a carefully worked out theological basis of the relationship between gospel and law, sacrament and life, grace and ethical instructions. The humanities are increasingly being taken seriously in the whole of theology, and particularly in pastoral and moral theology. There is fundamental acceptance of the necessity of inculturation and of a consequent plurality that arises from that of ways of looking at things and of emphases, of diversity in unity with loyally nurtured dialogue and along with this a process of continual learning. A fresh turning to the best that has been said in our own Western tradition about *epikeia* and the salutary use of the law helps at least partially as a remedy against too undifferentiated an application of the letter of the law to varied situations that can only with difficulty be compared to one another. It is in part a turning towards "the law of the Spirit of life in Christ Jesus" (Rm 8:2).

And not least I take courage and confidence in the future of our Church because of an ecumenical humility that is growing in many places: the awareness that even for the Roman Catholic Church there is much that it can and must learn from other sectors and traditions of Christendom. From many sides I nevertheless hear the objection: "Don't you see the centralism that is now running out of control

37

again?" Indeed, there are certain tendencies I observe with anxiety, but I also observe the opposing forces that are stronger and I trust in the good will on all sides.

To sum up, we should venture to put forward the following thesis, even if expressed cautiously. The Catholic Church is not tied for better or worse to its overstrict practice to date. The thorough study of the different traditions within Christendom and also within the Roman Catholic Church, the careful study of the relevant passages of Scripture, the understanding that today is confirmed ecumenically of "law and grace", of faith and grace on the one hand and law on the other, the understanding that has grown in the whole of Christendom and especially in recent Catholic theology of sacrament in general and of marriage as a sacrament in particular[8] – all these factors provide the Catholic Church with the space for a pastoral re-orientation such as is suggested by the contemporary situation in very many parts of the world and by the best anthropological insights.

3

The hoped-for new vision –
the spirituality and practice of
oikonomia

The courageous renewal of theology in almost all its branches, patient scholarly research, a pastoral approach and attitude, and the courage to accept and undertake dialogue, and to work through conflict: these, it must be hoped, will bear rich fruit despite all opposition. Today the Catholic Church has a number of qualified theologians of all specialities and tendencies that probably exceeds the number of theologians of the past eighteen or nineteen centuries. Our bishops and pastors have a higher level of education than ever. There also prevails greater freedom than in previous generations. Much has been more or less worked out theologically already, and indeed not less by the main body of believers than by the experts. Never before has the Church even approached having a similarly educated and theologically alert laity. In fact, on important matters, including that with which we are particularly occupied at present, our active believers are no longer "laymen" or "laywomen". They are growing up to greater maturity with an increasing awareness of distinctions. The *sensus fidelium* of the whole people of God, on which, despite everything, Cardinal Newman placed so much weight in his day, has today an undreamed-of dynamism, with greater competence and greater openness and honesty.

All this gives me the courage to have confidence. I dare to hope that the spirituality and the practice of the Orthodox Churches, enriched and fertilized and perhaps also purified by our own tradition and by new processes of learning, will to a considerable extent determine the landscape of our Church on the question of divorce and remarriage, and not in this field alone.

1. *What does the spirituality of* oikonomia *mean?*

The principle of *oikonomia* or economy of salvation occupies a distinguished place in the preparatory work for an eventual pan-Orthodox Council and in ecumenical conversations between the Orthodox Churches and Rome or the Churches and confessions that have emerged from the Reformation. I have no intention of going into the entire spectrum of the question here. That would need a comprehensive treatment with a great deal of scholarly apparatus. Others are occupied with looking after this need. Here all that needs to be said is what is most important for our subject.

"Economy" means the entire order of salvation of God as the benevolent father of the household and a spirituality that is marked by praise of the Church's all-merciful "steward" or "householder" and by trust in the "good shepherd" who knows and calls each and every one by name and when necessary leaves the ninety-nine healthy sheep behind for a while and astonishes them in order to go lovingly after a single lost sheep to rescue it. The spirituality and practice of economy are not conceivable at all in the Eastern Churches without their carefully tended theology and spirituality of the Holy Spirit. This builds on faith in the Holy Spirit, the paraclete, the comforter who makes everything that is good possible, the spirit of truth who lovingly leads us into the truth proclaimed by Jesus in his love and pastoral care. It is a question of trusting faith in the Holy Spirit who, if we devote ourselves completely to the praise of God and pray humbly, teaches us wisdom and the gift of discernment, who reveals commandment and law to us completely within the perspective of the order of grace. In the foreground in all this is the conviction that the letter without the spirit can only kill. "Economy" is a much more broadly understood concept and a spirituality which includes and decodes the best of our Western statements about *epikeia* but goes far beyond these.

In the spirituality and practice of economy the charisma of monks and hermits, who want to let themselves be led entirely by the Spirit and devote themselves to the praise of God, is joined to the simple piety of priests engaged in pastoral work, most of whom are married. It is a mutual supplementing of each other's gifts. To them economy is not conceivable at all without firm belief in the vocation of everyone to holiness, in remaining always open to the "law of the Spirit of life in Christ".

In the great tradition of the Orthodox Church there is no "scientific" theology separated from the eucharist and the gratuitousness of Christian life experienced in the eucharist. There are regulations and systems of discipline that do in part go into detail, but they are never separated from the all-embracing spirituality and practice of economy, from the out and out trinitarian piety that lives on the basis of economy.

2. *The application of economy to the doctrine of the indissolubility of marriage*

It is part of general theological knowledge that the statements of the Council of Trent about the indissolubility of marriage willed by God and proclaimed by Christ were only accepted when assurance was provided that this did not mean the condemnation of the Eastern Churches' practice of economy.

It is hardly to be assumed that at that time at Trent many Council Fathers thought the practice of economy should be considered in the Roman Catholic Church too. At the Council of Tent the Church was concerned to defend its own practice that had prevailed since the time of Pope Alexander III in the twelfth century and that in practice forbade every divorced person to remarry and indeed made such remarriage impossible through the introduction of the obligatory canonical form of marriage. The condemnation was directed against those who simply took the view that the Church (of Rome) erred when it taught that marriage was indissoluble. The ban on remarriage was included with this, even if imprecisely.

If today we are asking for a fresh reconsideration of the Church's practice, this does not involve claiming that the Church erred at that time, nor even that it erred in its practice. At that time it could well have been the best possible approach to this burning problem, in the circumstances of the time and given the defective knowledge then prevailing of the Church's own tradition. In any case the statements of the Council of Trent leave dogmatic space open for the existential question of what the Western Church in an age of ecumenism, can learn on this and similar questions from the spirituality and practice of the Orthodox Churches, and what best serves its pastoral mission in the world of today or indeed in considerable parts of the Catholic Church in order to show itself loyal to the father of the household who is able to link old and new from his divine treasury of wisdom.

After this essential comment we now need to consider as briefly as possible the practice of economy with regard to divorce and remarriage. The first thing to be emphasized is that the Eastern Churches have been inventive and imaginative in good forms of preparation and in moving forms of worship in order to instruct people in and guide them towards indissoluble faithfulness in marriage. The second is that it is no less important to see that in their best traditions the Orthodox Churches have made every effort to heal marriages that can be healed, above all in instruction in and guidance towards healing forgiveness, which indeed has been and is an essential point of their spirituality of economy. The question that torments us Western Christians, whether a marriage was validly contracted or can be declared invalid because of some deficiency, hardly came into view. There were no marriage tribunals in the Western sense. They just did not fit into their framework, into their mental outlook, culture and spirituality. If things of this kind existed they originated from the West.

(a) "Till death us do part"

In the mainstream Orthodox Churches, the physical death of a husband or wife means only a very partial "separation" from a dearly loved spouse. Widowers or widows moulded by the outlook of their Church took the Lord's saying: "He who is able to receive this, let him receive it" (Mt 19:12) very seriously, and Christians examined themselves to see if they could take it. But part of the counselling provided in the spirit of economy by the bishop, *starets* (an older monk acting as a spiritual director), or parish priest was the question whether in the actual situation remarriage might not be indicated for some good reason or other, for example for the sake of the children's upbringing and education. Orthodox Christians thus entered a second marriage as it were reluctantly, because they felt themselves linked by strong religious bonds to their departed spouse. The nurture of these strong religious bonds did indeed belong to the entire spirituality of economy, to training and encouraging people in faithful love even beyond the grave. But this never led to the enslavement of consciences. What was endorsed was what Paul had written: "A wife is bound to her husband as long as he lives. If the husband dies, she is free to be married to whom she wishes, only in the Lord. But in my judgement she is happier if she remains as she is. And I think that I have the Spirit of God" (1 Cor 7:39-40).

(b) The "moral death" of a marriage

In the Orthodox Churches the moral death of a marriage is regarded as something much more serious and radical than the death of a spouse, that is, than the ending of living together through physical death. The "moral death" of a marriage is the total destruction, the extremely painful collapse of a marriage intended to be indissoluble.

Just as in contemporary medicine the moment of physical death cannot be established as simply as perhaps it had been hoped, so there existed and exist not insignificant difficulties over determining the final destruction of a marriage. According to the proper practice of economy everything will be done to prevent the moral death of a marriage as long as a genuine hope exists of its survival.

What is regarded as "moral death"? Certainly not a single act of adultery. While Roman Catholic canonists and casuists have at some times and in some places maintained that a woman whose husband has committed adultery has the right to refuse to sleep with him ever again, and could in due course obtain a separation a *mensa et toro* (from bed and board), though, of course, without remarrying, in the Eastern Churches there have been hardly any advocates worth mentioning of the view that single serious

44

offences against marital fidelity should be regarded as indicating the "moral death" of the marriage. The moral death of a marriage has been and is seen as existing when, after a serious disparity has become evident, living together is no longer compatible with a sacrament of salvation, for example if the free practice of religion for one spouse is made impossible by the other; or if one spouse is seduced or forced by the other into doing something seriously sinful; or if one seriously threatens the life or physical and mental integrity of the other, and in similar cases, provided there is moral certainty that a change can no longer be hoped for. Briefly, moral death is accepted as having taken place when there is no longer within this marriage any potential of salvation, indeed when living together in fact works against the salvation and integrity of the other partner. It will be clear to everyone that here a non-ritual concept of sacramentality is integrated into an all-embracing vision of the total sacramentality of the Christian economy of salvation.

The moral death of a marriage is first diagnosed – in counselling – if its resuscitation at the level of the economy of salvation can no longer realistically be hoped for. For this reason there is no question of a hasty second marriage. A period of mourning is needed, a time for healing deep wounds. In particular, if a possible even if not grave sin on the part of the spouse whose salvation and integrity was threatened was not excluded, at least two years were expected of mourning and penance.

After the moral death of a marriage with all the extremely painful hurt involved, the admonition to celibacy ("he who is able to receive this, let him receive it") did not come so strongly into the picture for the spirituality of the Orthodox Church as in the case of the physical death of a dearly loved faithful spouse. Once again it is the therapeutic dimension of Eastern spirituality that is noticeably in the foreground. Someone who has lost a spouse through the moral death of the marriage needs our profoundest sympathy, and this must not be obscured in the event of possibly justified help being given to spouses to admit to themselves and to God their possible failure and to learn from it.

(c) The "psychic death" of the spouse

Today in the West the social sciences talk of the "social death" experienced in our civilization by the old, the weak, those who are no longer productive, when they are virtually excluded as if they no longer exist for us. This is one of the great evils of our civilization of welfare and success and a wrong development. It is especially the mentally ill who are found among those who all too easily suffer "social death".

In the best tradition of the Eastern Churches mental illness was a "holy" disease: with regard to the person who was mentally ill people felt they were being quite particularly accosted by Christ, and the same attitude was, by the way, adopted by all the saints of our own tradition. But what is something quite different is the question whether married life is something that can reasonably be expected, indeed whether it is at all possible at the level of the sacrament of salvation, with someone who is completely insane and severely mentally ill. In the eighteenth century several moralists maintained that a wife had to accede to the demands for sexual intercourse of her mentally ill husband so that his semen was not wasted: being ignorant of the woman's ovum, people saw in semen the *homunculus*, a tiny man in miniature. I have never become aware of this kind of view in the Eastern Churches. There, intercourse with someone who was completely unbalanced by mental illness was simply seen as absolutely unreasonable.

46

And they went on to accept that in this case a mutual married relationship could no longer be sacramental with the power to heal and save.

As far as the West is concerned it is known that St Boniface asked Rome if a married man whose wife was mentally ill and of unsound mind might take a second wife if complete abstinence seemed impossible to him. This was allowed by Rome under Gregory II as a concession, though with the admonition that the duty of looking after the mentally ill wife must not be neglected. It is quite to be expected from our Western tradition that the question whether a wife for her part might be able to marry again has not surfaced publicly. In the Orthodox tradition, on the other hand, "psychic death" is something that can affect husband and wife equally. Naturally great care was taken to establish whether such mental illness was irreversible and whether it had reached a stage that made a married relationship impossible at the level of the potential for salvation and a genuine loving relationship. And, of course, the duty of the family to look after the person who was mentally ill was not forgotten. It was, however, quite another thing whether this duty fell to the spouse or to the extended family of the sick person.

In the course of the last few decades very many Church marriage tribunals have accepted that mental illness (particularly certain specific forms of mental illness) that break out after a marriage has been contracted were present at least latently beforehand and thus affected the person's consent at the time of getting married, and that the marriage could therefore be declared invalid. Once again the difference needs to be underlined with the practice of economy. In that case one does not ask if the marriage was validly contracted or not but whether the marriage has finally been made impossible as a human relationship with potential for salvation through the full and incurable erup-

47

tion of mental illness. The decision based on the principle of economy can be very much more difficult than a declaration of invalidity by a Catholic marriage tribunal, and can demand longer delays; but in the foreground is the duty of saving love. And in the face of mental illness how great and wonderful can be a totally therapeutic church community along with a spouse totally committed to healing and salvation.

(d) "Civil death"

By "civil death" we mean, for example, an official declaration of death in the case of someone missing without trace. The concept in the practice of economy is more extensive. It was indeed recognized by Rome in a special form, in the case of people carried off into slavery who could not have any hope of finding again at some future time or place the spouses from whom they had been torn away. They were allowed by Rome to marry again, and if against all expectation the original spouse turned up again, the second marriage was what counted, while the other partner was also able to marry again. This is in itself a typical solution based on the principle of economy. But it does not have exactly the same effect as in the Eastern Churches because it is not in the contest of an entire spirituality of economy. In view of the many people who were found to be missing after the last World War, Catholic pastoral work was in considerable embarrassment about whether and when and under what conditions the remaining spouse of someone who had gone missing might be allowed a second marriage. I fully understand the fact that a strict tutiorism was followed here: people wanted to prevent the unutterable suffering that would occur if someone did turn up again.

In a wide sector of the tradition of economy, lifelong

imprisonment after a correspondingly heinous offence also counts as "civil death" to the extent that married life is no longer possible. Personally I regard it as a quite especially moving sign of genuine "sacramentality" in the way people live if the spouse of someone condemned to life imprisonment or a sentence of twenty years or more remains linked to that person in loving care. Everything needs to be done too so that in serving a sentence the spouse is not simply excluded from family life.

It is another question whether, on the basis of thinking out the principle of economy in a way that is true to life, the continuation of a marriage is still something that can reasonably be expected – and indeed not on the basis of a particular charisma but as a legal requirement – especially when what it involved is someone whose crime is marked by cruelty.

3. *The blessing of a second marriage in the form influenced by economy*

Although as long as the highest authority of the Church forbids it we cannot be allowed to adopt the form that the spirituality of economy has developed of blessing a second marriage after the collapse of what, according to our tradition, is a valid first marriage, it seems necessary to me for our grasp of the whole of what is involved to indicate a particular trait of such a Church blessing. Within the worldwide Orthodox Church there exists a certain diversity of rites, but one thing is common to all of them: the failed first marriage is sorrowfully recalled; the emphasis is on God's patience and mercy; it is made clear that one is not insisting on a right but has to thank god for his benevolent and healing economy of salvation. The gift of peace from above is explicitly prayed for.

49

The liturgical invitation to the contrite heart to praise God is moving, as for example, in the following prayer from the solemnization of a second marriage:

"Lord, have mercy."

"O Master, Lord our God, who showest pity upon all men, and whose providence is over all thy works; who knowest the secrets of man, and understandest all men: purge away our sins, and forgive the transgressions of thy servants, calling them to repentance, granting them remission of their iniquities, purification from their sins, and pardon of their errors, whether voluntary or involuntary. O thou who knowest the frailty of man's nature, in that thou art his Maker and Creator; who didst pardon Rahab the harlot, and accept the contrition of the Publican: remember not the sins of our ignorance from our youth up. for if thou wilt consider iniquity, O Lord, Lord, who shall stand before thee? Or what flesh shall be justified in thy sight? For thou only art righteous, sinless, holy, plenteous in mercy, of great compassion, and repentest thee of the evils of men. Do thou, O Master, who hast brought together in wedlock thy servants, N. and N., unite them to one another in love: vouchsafe unto them the contrition of the Publican, the tears of the Harlot, the confession of the Thief; that, repenting with their whole heart, and doing thy commandments in peace and oneness of mind, they may be deemed worthy also of thy heavenly kingdom.

"For thou are he who ordereth all things, and unto thee do we ascribe glory..."

This is followed by the invocation of peace and the invitation: "Bow your heads unto the Lord." Then comes what is probably the most characteristic prayer, one that makes it obvious how second marriages are marked by the whole concept of economy:

"O Lord Jesus Christ, the Word of God, who wast lifted up on the precious and life-giving cross, and didst thereby destroy the handwriting against us, and deliver us from the

50

dominion of the devil: cleanse thou the iniquities of thy servants; because they, being unable to bear the heat and burden of the day and the hot desires of the flesh, are now entering into the bond of a second marriage, as thou didst render lawful by thy chosen vessel, the Apostle Paul, saying, for the sake of us humble sinners, 'It is better to marry in the Lord than to burn.' Wherefore, inasmuch as thou art good and lovest mankind, do thou show mercy and forgive. Cleanse, put away, pardon our transgressions; for thou art he who didst take our infirmities on thy shoulders; for there is none sinless, or without uncleanness for so much as a single day of his life, save only Thou, who without sin didst endure the flesh, and bestowest on us passionlessness eternal."

"For thou art God, the God of the contrite in heart, and unto thee do we ascribe glory, to the Father, and to the Son, and to the Holy Spirit, now, and ever, and unto ages of ages."

It will be noted that, alongside the clear and perhaps over-clear reference to the couple's failure, the priest and the entire congregation join in the confession of their sinfulness and the plea for mercy. And everything flows again and again into praise of the All-merciful.[9]

The liturgical celebration of a second marriage must be seen as part of the whole process of the application of the principle of economy, which again and again concludes in praise of the all-merciful and all-holy "father of the household" (oicónomoz). Those seeking and those giving advice together look for the greatest possible faithfulness towards the precept of indissoluble marriage, but totally within the framework of the more comprehensive precept: "Be merciful, even as your Father is merciful" (Lk 6:36). Not only at the actual solemnization of a second marriage but throughout its entire course those involved are continually aware that we are all dependent on the healing and merciful love of the divine "father of the household".

As long as meaningful hope exists that a rickety marriage can be rescued, the fruitful tensions between the immediate precept of indissoluble marriage and the more comprehensive precept of being the image of the all-merciful God is probably the most powerful motive for mutual forgiveness and better understanding in the face of the All-merciful. I think that this spirituality and practice of economy works more effectively towards the durability of marriage and towards peace than legal rigidity, especially when in the predominant institution of the marriage tribunal the severity of the law is detached from the precept of mercy and leads many people to rebellion against an all too legalistic Church and, unfortunately, also against the norm of the indissolubility of marriage when it is understood in this way.

4

How in our Church can we reach a practice based on the principle of economy?

1. *The priority of a spirituality based on the principle of economy*

Simply to press ahead and to solve our urgent problems by using the methods of the Eastern Churches goes against the grain of our Church and can hardly lead us to the goal. Within the framework of our Church we must show it a credible loyalty on every stretch of the way. But it is not with an unimaginative but with a creative loyalty that we honour Christ's Church. We shall enter fully into the ecumenical dynamism of our own Church if both individually and as a community we make our own and internalize as much as possible the Orthodox Churches' spirituality of economy, in our personal piety, in catechesis, in preaching, in our spirituality stamped by eucharistic worship.

In this what cannot be overlooked – and we should not do so – is that a spirituality enriched by the Eastern tradition is already on its way. It is our indispensable duty to work in our Church for a healthy and strong public opinion in favour of an ecumenism that is lived. To this belongs not only an unpolemical understanding of other traditions but also a high degree of readiness to learn and of humility, so that, keeping the gospel in view, we may re-integrate into our theological thinking and into our piety valuable elements of what was originally a common tradition. We must do everything, and we want to do everything, to convince our bishops, priests and faithful that we enrich ourselves if we let ourselves be enriched by the great tradition of the Eastern Churches and learn from it.

If in the question of economy with regard to those who are divorced, and also in our moral and pastoral theology, we show ourselves open-minded and grateful, this takes a weight off the minds of our Orthodox brothers and sisters. In the prospect of a full reconciliation and reunion of the two sister Churches they are understandably afraid of a Roman centralism that goes hand in hand with efforts to regulate everything uniformly by law, looking at the effective control exercised by the congregations and tribunals of the Roman curia.

I would like to say openly here why this point is of such concern to me. At the time of Pope Paul VI and Patriarch Athenagoras I was friends in Rome with an Orthodox artist and journalist whose confirmation sponsor was Patriarch Athenagoras. The latter entrusted my friend with the task of letting me read an important letter in which this wonderful Patriarch expressed his profound admiration for Pope Paul VI and his own resolve to do everything for re-union. But he also spoke of the widespread fears within the Orthodox Churches. He was quite explicit in stating his conviction that a final reconciliation was not thinkable if Rome did not convincingly express its approval of the principle of economy, including its application to the divorced.

In the papal stand against contraception the Patriarch saw no problem for the Orthodox tradition, since they too were against contraception, while they were, of course, able to solve all cases of hardship sensibly with the tried and tested principle of economy; and this occurred in counselling. But what was much more decisive for them was the question of economy with regard to those who were divorced or deserted and whose first marriage was dead without any hope of revival.

2. *Psychotherapy in the spirit of the spirituality of economy*

Nothing stops us even today letting the spirit of economy prevail in our understanding of the sacrament of Penance and in the practice of confession. This concern coincides with certain forms of psychotherapeutic counselling.

We fulfil our function of counselling in the service of Christ's healing love if we do not unilaterally dictate a legal solution or obligation but pay attention to the pulse of the conscience of the person we are dealing with, respecting and sharing their conscience in the spirit of Vatican II's pastoral constitution (*Gaudium et spes* §16): "In fidelity to conscience, Christians are joined with the rest of men in the search for truth, and for the genuine solution to the numerous problems which arise in the life of individuals and from social relationships."

In the psychotherapeutic counselling of divorced people who either have already remarried or are considering doing so, we shall follow a fundamental insight of Viktor Frankl and other psychotherapists: instead of simply confronting people with a norm, say the norm that corresponds to our conscience or is simply the general norm of the Church, we shall listen patiently to how our opposite numbers themselves seek the way to the depth of their own conscience and to what their motives and reasons are. By listening with an alert conscience (*con-scientia* – existentially experienced knowledge in union with the other) and carefully examining the possibilities, we shall help them in an honest search for enlightenment. Our words, our gestures, our

55

face should encourage, rather than betray reproach and irritation. It should always be a word of that love that quite simply is the truth.

In such situations of respecting and sharing in an examination of conscience we shall as Christians live in full awareness of the presence of the Holy Spirit, the comforter, the enabler, the Spirit of truth, and trust that, if we listen to each other in love, he will be at work in everyone and for everyone. Our primary awareness is thus not of a legal norm but of the gracious working of the Holy Spirit. That is a genuine expression of the cast of mind of economy.

This kind of combination of the spirituality of economy with the fundamental rules of healing love (cf. for example logotherapy) will prove worthwhile in the often difficult process of mourning after the collapse of a marriage, in working through hurtful experiences and, where this is the case, coming to terms with one's own failure, and finally, when those who are divorced consider what in their actual situation could be the best or at least not the worst. If at the conclusion of counselling or therapy of this kind the person concerned comes to the conscientious judgement that the best thing for him or her and for his or her children would be to think of getting married again, then as representatives of the Church we cannot in fact directly confirm this, as would correspond to the procedure of Orthodox counselling on the basis of economy; but we shall express our respect for his or her honest decision in conscience. What cannot be avoided in this is touching on the question of how the Church community and the person's parish priest are likely to react. Nevertheless we can point to the Eastern Churches' solution based on the principle of economy and give our modest opinion whether our opposite number's decision corresponds or not to the basic principle of economy.

If it is a question of divorced people living happily in a second marriage who only then come to believe or return to the faith, while at the time of the broken first marriage they either did not belong to the Church at all or were completely alienated from it, then we can find a solution which corresponds both to the attitude of economy and to our own best tradition. If therefore they come to us while they are and have for the whole time been living in good faith in the second marriage, then in my view a solution on the basis of *epikeia* is possible and/or a solution in the internal forum (cf. p. 75 below). I know that many bishops and even cardinals have already been convinced that this is the right approach and have acted in this way. The deeper we grow into the spirituality of economy and the better we get to know the breadth of our own tradition, the more convincingly and healingly shall we be able to help.

On the other hand we cannot, at least in the meantime, go as far as blessing the second marriage in the sense of the Eastern Churches' principle of economy. This is forbidden us and is also not necessary, even though it would often be desired in itself.

5

First steps towards a reform of the law

1. *Overcoming a harsh tutiorism in the Church's nullity procedure*

An important step in the spirit of economy and in the direction of a procedure in keeping with this would in my view be to make equity an effective component of the Church's nullity procedure. This would not in any case be any revolutionary innovation but a step that corresponds to the present sense of justice and equity within the Church and within society as a whole. What is involved is nothing more and nothing less than the long overdue surmounting of a harsh tutiorism with regard to a doubtful validity of the first marriage.

In the tough fight against Jansenism and rigorism the Church has overcome this legalistic tutiorism, but not, however, with regard to weighing up the tension between law and freedom in the case of the extremely doubtful validity of a marriage that has collapsed beyond hope.

The tutiorism of rigoristic moralists maintained that, in a conflict between freedom and an obligation of a legal nature the existence of which was in doubt, especially when what was involved was possibly a divine commandment or one of the natural law, freedom must recede to the point of the non-existence or non-application of the law being unequivocally demonstrated without any doubt.

Behind this stood the false conviction that doing good and acting in accordance with the law coincided completely. The rigorists did not see any space for creative freedom. In their view the Christian should only do what is explicitly allowed by the law.

It was above all St Alphonsus who fought against the tutiorist constriction of Christian freedom. His chief argument was that God had not begun by establishing commandments and prohibitions and creating a human being for these: on the contrary, God created man for freedom and gave him commandments and prohibitions to protect true freedom: "For God has called us to peace" (1 Cor 7:15).

Tutiorism crushes man's creative freedom for what is good. It leads to revolt against a law that is experienced as intolerable. Together with St Alphonsus all reputable moral theologians and pastors maintain that it is wrong to heap legal burdens on to people when it is not sufficiently established that such burdens are willed by God in this way. It is also a sin against the proper proclamation of salvation to demand fulfilment of a legal requirement under pain of mortal sin if such a requirement cannot be unequivocally demonstrated or made comprehensible. These basic principles are generally recognized today in moral theology as a whole, but not in the field of sexual morality with regard to the obligation of celibacy after the collapse of a doubtfully valid marriage.

In many cases the Church's marriage tribunals still demand today one hundred per cent proofs and documentation as a condition for a nullity decree. Put the other way, this means that even on the basis of the flimsiest of doubts whether the first marriage was indeed valid the legal obligation of celibacy is "ordained" in such a case. Behind this tutiorism, this wanting to follow the safer path, stands the fear of possibly sinning against the sacramentality of marriage by tolerating a second marriage. In this way one arrives at applying the harshest enforcement of a legalistic tutiorism precisely in this most sensitive area. The otherwise unchallenged principle that the sacraments are made for man if forgotten, as is the even clearer principle that laws are for people and not people for extremely dubiously binding laws.

2. *Respecting the basic human right to marriage*

The harshness of this kind of legal practice and procedure was not nearly so much perceived in earlier times within European society as it is today; for because of the socio-economic structure not all those capable of marrying were for a long time able to marry. But single people and also those who were separated were looked after humanely within the extended family of that time.

Today the right to marriage and a family is experienced as one of the most fundamental human rights. The withholding of this right has in many cases catastrophic consequences for those who are on their own, especially for those who are divorced or deserted: alcoholism, dependence on drugs, indeed depression to the point of suicide. Nor should the Church's legislators be unaware that divorced people for whom a second marriage is impossible show a much higher suicide rate than those who have the security of marriage and a family. The Church, which presents itself as the champion of human rights, should "for the sake of our salvation" dissociate itself from a tutiorism that cannot be justified at all theologically.

In the face of a first marriage that is irrevocably "dead" there should be no ban on a second marriage in case of doubt about the original validity of the first. Rather, divorced people who are personally convinced that their first marriage was invalid from the start and destined to collapse should be free to marry again "in the Lord".

Nevertheless I would like to enter one reservation. If one of the spouses has behaved offensively in a way that contributed to the collapse of the marriage, he or she should be offered suitable therapy before being allowed a second marriage, and this even in the case of the probable invalidity of the first marriage – for his or her own good and the good of any eventual future spouse.

I would like to illustrate this by a case known to me personally. The Church annulled the marriage of a homosexual man who paraded his homosexual leanings and activity in a way that was tremendously hurtful to his wife. For the innocent wife this meant freedom to marry. The man, however, was forbidden to marry until he overcame his homosexuality. The shock induced the man to undergo therapy which finally proved to be successful, as his therapist confirmed. My reservation thus remains within the field of Our Lord's saying: "I came not to judge... but to save" (Jn 12:47).

3. *On whom does the burden of proof fall?*

Up till now the burden of proof fell on the divorced person or the innocent deserted spouse, and that to an incredibly excessive degree. According to my proposal the burden of proof for validity would fall predominantly on the Church's marriage tribunal.

It ought not to block a second marriage without bringing forward good reasons for the validity of the first marriage, and at least to the extent that a possible ban on marriage should not in any way have the character or appearance of arbitrariness.

From experience I know that often one of the judges of

the marriage tribunal has let himself be convinced of the invalidity of the first marriage while another, who has to share in the decision, is fiercely opposed to an annulment on the ground of a doubt that has not yet been cleared up. In that case no nullity decree is issued. Not infrequently a marriage is declared invalid after careful examination by a first tribunal, and after some time the appeal tribunal declares that the invalidity has not been established, often indeed on the basis of a clear appeal to tutiorism. In such cases the basic right to marriage and a family should be protected by the legislator.

Of course, in the case of a change in the law of this kind care must be taken that the reform is implemented by competent personnel. Thorough grounding is needed not only in Canon Law but also in the humanities and in psychotherapy in order for the principle "Law is for man, not man for the law" to be made properly effective.

The Church needs competent pastoral care for the divorced. It is necessary to heal many festering wounds. There is considerable need for serious therapeutic help so that a possible second marriage stands a better chance. I would also advocate that second marriages should not be solemnized with great ceremony in church but rather with due simplicity.

For the organic transition to and the arrangements for this kind of re-evaluation of the right to marriage and a family we could learn from the experiences of other parts of Christendom. I am thinking first of all of the Churches or confessions that emerged from the Reformation of the sixteenth century: for a long time they did indeed have a marriage discipline similar to that of our Church but then sought other ways of giving effect to the fundamental right to marriage in such a way that the fundamental indissolubility of marriage was not denied and the trend to divorce was resisted to the best of their ability.

63

It should, however, be clear to the reader that the proposed reform does not yet signify a genuine adaptation to the Eastern Churches' practice of economy. It would be merely an overdue modification of the discipline of our own Church. But it could of course be a significant step in the direction of the Orthodox Churches' principle of economy if we do not lose sight of the spirituality based on this principle.

6

What can be done today in advance of any reform of the law?

1. *Relapse into legalism or pressing forward at the wrong time?*

Once again I would like to remind the reader that it is not my intention to invite anyone to rebel against or even simply to ignore the Church's present discipline. We are occupied with two different questions, even if they are related to each other. First, what reform of the Church's formulation of doctrine and discipline do we regard as sensible and desirable? We have gone into this above. The second question which will occupy us in what follows is: how can we act sensibly on the basis of the Church's present discipline and guidelines? The question is one that has to be faced by bishops, by all who are active in pastoral work and counselling and, of course, directly by those who are divorced, deserted, or remarried.

I would, however, ask the reader only to read this part of the book after having carefully read the preceding chapters. He or she can then form a personal judgement whether what follows breathes the same spirit as the previous remarks, or whether the author is perhaps relapsing into too legalistic a pattern of thought. Others will rather ask themselves whether what is to be said now does justice to the Church's doctrine and discipline. I can only assure my readers that it is my honest intention to keep an eye on both dangers and thus neither to relapse into too legalistic a pattern of thought nor to undermine just laws. My concern is to invite everyone to strive towards being able to say with the Apostle of the Gentiles: "To those under the law I became as one under the law – though not being myself under the law – that I might win those under the law. To those outside the law I became as one outside the law – not being without law toward God but under the law of Christ – that I might win those outside the law" (1 Cor 9:20-21).

In this I am also thinking of helping towards the Church being able to win over for reunion those parts of Christendom (the Orthodox Churches, the Reformed Churches) who are not impressed by our marriage law and discipline as they have been up till now. I am also thinking of the evangelization of those parts of humanity whose quite different civilization and structure of marriage hardly key them into our Western discipline and practice on these questions. For this very reason I ask the well-disposed reader to gauge my prudent endeavours and my advice against the passage from St Paul quoted above and also against the Apostle's concern that is expressed in the same letter to the Corinthians in connection with the discipline to be followed in marriage questions: "For God has called us to peace" (1 Cor 7:15).

2. What in any case we should do or refrain from doing

All should be aware that what we are very seriously concerned with in the whole of Christian life and especially in the marriage bond is the fundamental virtue of loyalty and fidelity. We must never forget that Christ sealed the new and eternal covenant with his own blood. His merciful love on the cross has reconciled us and is for us an invitation that presses on us from within to serve him ever more loyally and faithfully, to get to know his gospel ever better and to translate it into action, in fact in forgiveness and in the readiness to forgive, since we all live on the basis of God's forgiveness. Marriage as the sacrament of salvation for the couple and the sign of salvation for their children and the world around is worth the sacrifice of sticking it out and, if it has begun to crumble, putting it together again.

Those who are divorced or deserted should strive with all their might to believe in God's faithful love even after such shattering experiences and to bear witness to it. Not infrequently on the basis of their own experience they should and can help other married people who have reached a crisis to overcome this crisis sensibly and, if at all possible, to persevere in their married relationship and possibly in due course to seek assistance from experienced pastors, counsellors, or psychotherapists.

As statistics show, a considerable proportion of those who have divorced openly admit that their marriages could have been saved. To acknowledge this is an act of humility and a precious encouragement for others. It is in cooperation with divorced people who, through their own bitter experience, have won through to profound awareness and maturity and who may well come together in self-help groups that pastors can often find the best way of approaching married couples in crisis and can effectively advise and encourage them.

We shall combine all our forces to strive against that trend that would like to represent divorce and remarriage as something normal. But in our zeal we shall carefully avoid pouncing on married couples in crisis with a harsh reminder that "thou shalt" or "thou shalt not": nor shall we bring out ready-prepared answers even before we have listened sensitively to what people have to say. We should encourage them to talk things out themselves, to give expression to their feelings, openly to expound their own reflections.

3. *Psychotherapeutic efforts at reconciliation*

As long as we have reason to hope that a marriage can be healed and strengthened we shall express this hope of ours, albeit with circumspection, and encourage those concerned to hope themselves. Since many married couples in crisis are sent to me by others, I have gradually developed a kind of method that I would like to tell the reader about here.

First of all I receive each spouse separately and let him or her talk undisturbed. Very carefully at first I suggest that they should tell me the good sides which their spouse used to display and to some extent still does today. In this there is already in the background an effort to heal their memories. I pay careful attention to which of the two still has a good memory of the other and is happy to remember his or her good sides.

Then I invite the two to a joint conversation. I start with a prayer suitable for the occasion and invite the couple to join me in silent or even oral prayer. Then I turn to the one who shows the most hopeful signs or at least has traces of happy memories and in words like these ask him or her to speak: "Mary, may I ask you to tell me in the presence of God and of your husband all the good you remember about him?" While she is talking, the other one's face often has a moving tale to tell – astonishment, enlightenment, perhaps (not infrequently) a first reaction: "But, Mary, why didn't you ever tell me that before?"

If the first speaker (whom I have specially prepared in advance for this) succeeds in fact in mentioning only the good points of the other, I thank God explicitly for these happy memories and turn to the other spouse:

"Now, Martin, I would like you for your part to tell us all the good things you remember about your wife."

If the other partner also succeeds in recalling the good things that they have stored up and experienced together, we pray, and through a period of silence I give the two some time to digest this often unexpected experience.

Then, if the situation has reached that point, a new step follows. I say something like: "You do not now need to make any confession of wrong-doing. I have heard enough of that already anyway. What is involved now is a new courageous step: away from accusations and complaints about the other towards accepting one's own dark side, one's own failure." Then we pray God together for forgiveness and healing. If the couple want it, I give them absolution.

The more clearly one refrains from dictating a solution to those involved and the more clearly they discern that one is humbly joining them in seeking God's will, the greater are the chances of being able to contribute to a reconciliation and healing.

The same applies undoubtedly when divorce or desertion is a *fait accompli* and counselling is concerned with whether – as someone on one's own – one can bear witness to indissoluble valid marriage or is thinking of remarrying. In this the psychotherapeutic dialogue cannot solely revolve around the question whether the first marriage was or was not valid. One must above all listen to what those concerned have to say about their own feelings, anxieties, expectations and hopes, and also to the extent to which they are inclined to "believe" in the Church's doctrine and its current discipline.

It is as well not to make directly for the ban on a second marriage. It is a question of sharing in in the divorced or deserted spouse's mourning for the marriage that was, suggesting motives for forgiveness, helping him or her to overcome the tendency to put all the blame on the other, to come to a peaceful agreement about financial interests and obligations, to think realistically of the good of the children. If the darkest clouds on these questions have dispersed, discussion of the possible consideration of a second marriage can become fruitful.

In any case those who are divorced, whether they are still single or have married again in a register office, should be fully aware that they are not excluded from the Church as if they were some kind of leper. They should be aware that we respect their conscience and that our help is aimed above all at their finding and following their own path themselves on the basis of a conscience that is awake and alert.

4. *To what extent should we encourage recourse to* epikeia *and to what extent should we tolerate it?*

Over the last few decades moral theologians and pastoral practice have rediscovered or at least given more room to the human and Christian virtue of *epikeia*. *Epikeia* is an important dimension of the virtue of prudence with regard to decisions where there is conflict of values, law or obligation. It is an essential pillar of an ethic of responsibility and of education towards Christian and human maturity. St Alphonsus of Liguori, the patron saint of moral theologians, teaches unequivocally: "*Epikeia* means the exception of a case because of the situation from which can be judged, with certainty or at least with sufficient probability, that the legislator did not intend to include it under the law. This *epikeia* has its place not only in human laws but also in natural laws where, because of the circumstances, the action could be freed from malice."[10] In no way can *epikeia* be suspected of being, or misinterpreted as, a kind of shirking in the face of important challenges, even though it also can be applied when someone is convinced that an unduly heavy burden is being demanded of him or her by the law or by the authorities.

The virtue of *epikeia* also serves the law and the legislator. According to Aristotle it is a virtue of the legislator and of the authorities, a virtue thanks to which these are ready to give room to *epikeia* with regard to legal regulation in the case of a law or regulation being unreasonably harsh or even damaging if it were followed literally (without presupposing the virtue of *epikeia*): the legislator does not wish to bring extraordinary situations within the letter of the law. And part of a healthy relationship between the subject on the one hand and law and the authorities on the other is that the former believes in the virtue of *epikeia* in the legislator and allows himself or herself the sensible application of *epikeia* in all cases without being afraid of being a criminal.

There are some extremely basic moral norms which have an absolute validity, as for example the golden rule: "Do to no one what you would not want done to you" (Tb 4:15).

It can have a disastrous effect on sound relationships to law and authority if state officials demand a literal observance of the law even in obviously hard cases. Similarly and to an even greater extent unhealthy tensions arise in the Church if with reference to the divinely instituted teaching authority a host of secondary or derived moral norms are declared to be valid without exception and not open to any application of *epikeia* and if with this an uncritical trust in the magisterium is strongly demanded as if in the past and in the present it had never erred and had never loaded people with heavy burdens.

71

The aversion to *epikeia* can be explained partly by an experience that confirms or is thought to confirm that whim and egoism or both drape themselves in the mantle of *epikeia*. It prevails everywhere that centralism or authoritarian forms of government have contributed to identifying unity with imposed uniformity.

Greater observance of *epikeia* in the Church of today is connected with the growing spirit of ecumenism. A better awareness of history and the spirit of ecumenism lead to the discovery in many fields not only of dogmatic theology but also of moral theology that we Catholics can learn not just something but quite a lot from the other parts of Christendom. Ecumenism does not thrive when people are not ready to learn and do not admit honestly that many formulations of doctrinal statements and moral norms are culturally and in some other way historically conditioned and have been able to be made harsher as a result of self-righteousness.

Epikeia is not needed with regard to the law of love and justice inscribed in the heart of man: this requires always the courageous action of love in keeping with the conscience. It is, on the contrary, the secondary, deduced norms of the natural moral law which are the result of joint experience and reflection that need *epikeia*. This, of course, applies even more when a norm has been arrived at without the best possible exchange of experience and reflection. The more detailed and numerous such norms are, the more frequently does one find a conflict of norms that can only be resolved by *epikeia*.

St Alphonsus of Liguori drew conclusions which are still relevant today from his view of *epikeia*. Thus, for example, he teaches, along with all the other moralists of his age, that the interruption of sexual intercourse is an offence against the goal of fertility, but adds: "It is morally permitted to interrupt sexual intercourse if a proportionate

72

reason [*justa causa*] exists".[11] Similarly he gave *epikeia* precedence over the Church's ban on interest, which got him into a lot of trouble with tutiorist and rigorists, and did the same in many other questions that are still burning problems today.

In preceding chapters we have seen that in the Orthodox Churches from the earliest times the natural virtue of *epikeia* has in questions of marriage been enveloped by the spirituality of economy, by praise of the all-merciful Father. We have much to learn from this spirituality, and it should and can protect us from the wrong application of *epikeia*. I would not, however, want simply to extend the concept of *epikeia* to cover the Eastern Churches' practice of economy. The starting-point to begin with is our much more restricted Western concept of *epikeia*, in which, however, I follow the more understanding interpretation in our Church, as for example that of St Alphonsus.

5. Epikeia *with regard to the practice of annulment*

The starting point of our casuistry with reference to *epikeia* is the case in which those concerned and also the pastor come to a clear judgement ("with a high degree of probability" as is demanded by St Alphonsus) that according to sound doctrine and a sound consideration of the Church's discipline the first marriage was invalid. The question of *epikeia* then arises above all when a declaration of nullity is only refused because all the proofs are not present, while those concerned – and after sufficient consideration the pastor too – are convinced that the first marriage was invalid from the start. By virtue of *epikeia* those concerned are then fundamentally justified in entering a second marriage. And in my view the pastor can then very quietly conduct the wedding ceremony.

73

Ought he to enter them in the wedding register or deal with them exclusively in the internal forum? In cases where the bishop of the diocese does not want to involve himself in the application of *epikeia* and also is not minded to tolerate it, there are probably three possibilities. First, the parish priest can accept a certain measure of risk himself in the readiness both to take responsibility for his actions and to bear any unpleasant consequences in a Christian spirit. The second possibility is for him to tell the couple who want to get married that in this situation they can have recourse to the canonical emergency form of marriage, that is before two witnesses, because no duly empowered priest is available.[12] A third option is that, after counselling from their parish priest and confessor, the couple regard their civil wedding as a substitute emergency form of marriage given the non-availability of a duly empowered priest and quite simply trust that with the grace of God they can live their second marriage in such a way that it approaches as perfectly as possible to the Christian ideal of marriage.

With not a few others I am also of the opinion that one of these three options can be applied according to circumstances if the decision of the marriage tribunal is being, has. been or in all likelihood will be delayed for years, but once again provided that those concerned are convinced ("with a high degree of probability") that their first marriage was invalid. If the Church's hierarchy takes the view that for the sake of justice it must examine the remarriage of divorced people who are convinced that their first marriage was invalid from the start, then it is obliged by justice not to lay any burdens that are too heavy on those concerned. I know personally of cases where a woman who was the innocent party in a divorce and whose first husband had categorically excluded having children has had to wait for years for the annulment of her first marriage by the Church's

74

marriage tribunals until eventually she had passed the age when she could hope to have a baby herself. Here there are apparent serious reasons both for the application of *epikeia* and for the duty of ensuring that in future nobody is faced with the difficult decision of either going on waiting or having to deal with the case by *epikeia*.

It should have become clear to the reader that solutions on the basis of *epikeia* are not solutions by means of an isolated and hidden decision by the individual conscience. Normally they are the fruit of careful advice and counselling, involving the pastor, and often through entries in Church registers they extend visibly into the external forum.

In what follows it is a question of decisions of conscience which as far as possible are dealt with in the internal forum of the Church's sacramental practice but at least to begin with do not reach the external field of law. This distinction is important.

6. *Solutions in the internal forum*

Very many cases which up until the twelfth century in the Roman Catholic Church were settled in the external legal sphere, as they still are in all the Orthodox Churches of the East, cannot today in our Church even be solved by *epikeia*, at least as long as this also involves the external legal sphere, provided we base ourselves loyally on the Church's present discipline.

In what follows we are concerned exclusively with marriages where there is neither a Church decree of nullity nor a dispensation (as in the case of unconsummated marriages or, where consummated marriages are concerned, in the case of the Pauline and Petrine privileges). In many ways the internal forum solution is similar to the economy solution of the Eastern Churches, but with two important restrictions: in the Eastern Churches the the external forum (making things clear in the field of the Church's public law) is also included, and at the same time its field of application is very much broader.

In our church, on the contrary, attempts to solve cases in the internal forum are restricted to the sacramental sphere protected by the seal of the confessional. This is, however, a sphere of great dignity. To this extent solutions in the internal forum go beyond mere decisions in conscience taken by an individual or a couple before God.[13]

I am thinking first of all of those heart-rending cases involving someone who is the innocent party in a divorce and has been deserted against his or her will, but I am also aware that there is a whole range of transitions with more or less failure or even guilt on the part of the person concerned.

I am thinking above all of those second marriages after a divorce or separation where the couple concerned have married, contrary to the Church's discipline, with heavy hearts because they thought they were protecting the education of young children or because for a number of reasons they did not think they were able to cope with life alone. Moreover, I am restricting my proposals to situations in which bringing the first marriage back to life is completely excluded.

We pastors and confessors see these people often years later, and not infrequently after what humanly speaking is a successful second marriage, the dissolution of which simply does not come into question for them. In many cases with which I have had to deal, the second marriage was for one or both partners a way back to faith or to a first conversion to faith. Some were burdened with the consciousness of guilt in having contracted an invalid marriage, at least one that was invalid in the eyes of the

Church; others, after a period of suffering pangs of conscience or of a disturbed conscience, came to the conviction, either by themselves or in discussion with valued advisers, that they had acted more or less rightly and were of the opinion that "God has blessed the second marriage" so that they no longer suffered any qualms of conscience. Thus in the field of conscience many have already completely sorted things out for themselves when they approach a confessor or pastor. Nearly all of them are concerned with receiving the sacraments of reconciliation and of the eucharist and in most cases – as far as my experience goes – this longing is very deeply-felt and genuine. What, however, cannot be excluded is that it usually arises in connection with the first communion of one of the children if additional encouragement is not otherwise provided. But this should not simply be devalued. One should consider what exclusion from the sacraments means to parents who bring their children up as Catholics and who experience all that their children's first communion means to them.

In not a few cases the question whether a return to the first spouse had been considered or would be possible would be quite out of place. It could be regarded not only as an unnecessary but also as an offensive demand. On the other hand the question of how the relationship with the first spouse has developed and whether a reconciliation and healing of the wounds has taken place is most often touched on by those concerned themselves.

Talking sensibly and compassionately on this is often part of the sacrament of reconciliation and of peace. The sacramental liberating experience of a forgiving God and a merciful Church easily becomes a new and strong reason to forgive injustice and also gradually to become ready to heal the other's wounds, to the extent that this is necessary and possible.

7. *How high must the requirements for absolution be?*

Before the Council a priest who in contravention of the law of celibacy and his own promises had got married could only be given absolution if he renounced all sexual intercourse with the mother of their children, the woman he had married in a civil ceremony, and if the couple thus lived together like brother and sister. I had to do with quite a lot of cases myself of repentant priests where this worked after a certain struggle, because the wife cooperated. In rigorist circles this formula was then extended to those who had divorced and remarried, who longed for the sacraments, but who for reasons of human and Christian responsibility could not and also did not want to dissolve the second marriage. Marriage counsellors, psychotherapists and pastors were up in arms against this and talked of laying impossible burdens on people. Bad experiences with this idea, with the cooperation of the moral theologians, led to it being in practice consigned to oblivion, at least in some countries. After the Council tensions arose in many local Churches because of great differences in pastoral practice. A tendency was detected of finding ways round the system of Church marriage tribunals that was not functioning well. In April 1973 the Congregation for the Doctrine of Faith therefore stepped in with a circular sent to all bishops and provided guidelines. Here we are interested above all in what these say about the internal forum solution:

"In regard to admission to the sacraments, local bishops are asked on the one hand to stress observance of current discipline, and on the other hand to take care that pastors of souls exercise special care to seek out those who are living in an irregular union by applying to the solution of such cases, in addition to other rightful means, the Church's approved practice in the internal forum."

At once there arose a debate as to whether "the Church's approved practice" meant the brother and sister formula or not. The US bishops asked the Congregation for the Doctrine of Faith for clarification. It is significant, and I find it encouraging, that the Congregation for the Doctrine of Faith did not wish to commit itself to that formula and condition. In a letter to Archbishop Joseph Bernardin of Cincinnati (now Archbishop of Chicago and a cardinal) it wrote:

"I would like to state now that this phrase must be understood in the context of traditional moral theology. These couples may be allowed to receive the sacraments on two conditions, that they try to live according to the demands of Christian moral principles and that they receive the sacraments in churches in which they are not known so that they will not create any scandal." [14]

It is noteworthy that there is no mention of specifying a brother and sister relationship in answer to this question. Clearly in view of the opinion of many moral theologians and therapists there was no wish to insist on this. The same tendency clearly predominated at the Roman Synod of Bishops on the family in 1980 but was given a more restrictive interpretation by the Pope in his closing address, and this was made even clearer in the apostolic exhortation *Familiaris consortio* that resulted from the synod. Admission to the sacraments is only allowed when "a man and a woman cannot satisfy the obligation to separate" but "take on themselves the duty to live in complete continence, that is, by abstinence from the acts proper to married couples" and when the danger of scandal does not exist (§84).

As far as the danger of scandal is concerned one must pay heed to existing conditions. In Germany, Austria and Switzerland the situation is such that by far the largest part of practising Catholics would instead be scandalized if innocent divorced people who have remarried were excluded from the sacraments. The following picture, for example, emerged from a survey among more than 6,000 readers of the Catholic magazine *Weltbild*. Asked whether someone who was the innocent party in a divorce and had subsequently remarried should be admitted to the sacraments, 88.6 per cent said such a person should, and only 11.4 per cent said the person should not.

In view of this conviction among the people of God and the equally undeniable ineffectiveness among contemporary people of promoting the stability of marriage by harsh measures against the innocent, the reference to the danger of scandal must have a different effect. The exclusion from the Church's sacraments of innocent parties to a divorce who are living in what humanly speaking is a good second marriage will today contribute hardly anything towards the strengthening loyalty to the indissoluble bond of marriage or strengthening Christians who are being tempted.

The exclusion of Christians who are honestly seeking the will of God in the situation in which they find themselves and who are fulfilling it to the best of their ability makes the Church less attractive and diminishes its ability to shine forth as the sacrament of God's mercy.

A discipline as harsh as this faces all of us with the question whether we have reason to regard ourselves as more righteous than these innocent divorced people who are living in a second marriage the destruction of which cannot be God's will or at any rate is not seen by those concerned as God's will and psychologically ought not to be seen as such.

If we do not wish to destroy the second marriage which now exists and which, in the conviction of the Orthodox and Protestant Churches, is seen as the sign of salvation of an all-merciful Father and which in fact contributes much to peace and guards against serious damage, then there is in this connection a statement of the Second Vatican Council which we must take no less seriously than what Pope John Paul II said in his apostolic exhortation. In the chapter on marriage and the family of its pastoral constitution on the Church in the Modern World (*Gaudium et spes* § 51), the Council says: "Where the intimacy of married life is broken, it often happens that faithfulness is imperilled and the good of the children suffers: then the education of the children as well as the courage to accept more children are both endangered."

Whatever position one adopts with regard to the restrictive interpretation of the traditional internal forum solution, in its application tried and tested principles of moral theology and pastoral practice should not be overlooked. I am referring here to St Alphonsus's oft-repeated and urgent warning that one should not put forward certain demands in confession if it is to be expected that these will confuse rather than enlighten the conscience so that a danger exists that material sin will turn into formal sin.

There are still, in my opinion, devout Christians among the divorced and remarried who are convinced that the Pope's norm, however harsh it may appear, is right.

In such cases it is once again a question of respecting their conscience instead of needlessly confusing it. One can and should encourage them and give them absolution, even if in all probability they are not, despite all their good will, living up to this norm: here too what applies is the general principle that good will is enough.

All of us all too often fail in things the loyal fulfilment of which is certainly God's will and is something we should find easier than total continence on the part of a man and wife who love each other.

8. *Reconciliation after the break-up of a marriage brought about by disgraceful behaviour*

In nearly all divorces there is a jumble of innocent failure, culpable failure and fateful tragedy that cannot be disentangled. To this must be added the failure of all the rest of us, which for many families and marriages in crisis may have no little crucial effect as a kind of environmental damage. This jumble and entanglement should not, however, blind us to the fact that often the final breakup of the marriage is simply endured by one spouse despite a high degree of readiness to forgive and an astonishing capacity for suffering. There is that large group of whom we can and must say in rather simplified terms that they are innocent parties to a divorce.

At the other extreme of the spectrum are such things as irresponsibly intervening in somebody else's marriage, breaking up one's own and other people's marriages in a way that causes the maximum offence, often with a second or third marriage to a spouse who has been seduced into adultery and culpably alienated from his or her original partner. Of course, we are aware that we can never look into the depths of someone's heart, but there are ways of behaving that profoundly unsettle trust and inflict great damage on the community, above all on the community of the Church. The offence often lies simply in the breaking up of a marriage that previously was sound, or of a marriage that was on the way to being healed.

Despite every caution, in view of the Lord's reminder "judge not", there are criteria for distinguishing between innocent and culpable divorce and indeed the breaking up of a marriage in a way that creates serious offence. The offence is compounded when there follows very soon after the divorce not merely a shacking up with the partner in crime (whose sin consists not just of individual acts but the

82

whole business of breaking up the marriage) but a formal civil wedding.

The Eastern Churches' discipline based on economy has worked out clear criteria for such cases. On average the culpable party of a divorce has roughly five years' penance and exclusion from the sacraments imposed on him or her, depending, of course, on the degree of offence that can be established. Then too the question still arises whether the person whose disgraceful behaviour led to the divorce should or must be required to separate from his or her accomplice in sin. In this context I have always been amazed that such a courageous prophet as Nathan should have tolerated David's cohabitation with Bathsheba after his adultery with her and his murder of her husband Uriah the Hittite.

After these preliminary considerations here now is my opinion with regard to reconciliation after a seriously culpable divorce that gives offence followed by an equally offensive civil second marriage – a tentative opinion that is seeking greater enlightenment. My view is that clear signs of repentance must be made:

(1) Whenever it is possible I think of the requirement of giving up the sinful connection at least in the case of the previous spouse being ready and able to forgive the unfaithful husband or wife and to resume married life with him or her in healing love. Unfortunately, this is often not possible.

(2) Injustice done to the innocent party in the divorce must be made good to the best of one's ability. His or her forgiveness must be patiently striven for, one's own guilt admitted. Ultimately it is a question of becoming involved as a mediator in the work of human reconciliation.

Naturally, material injustice must also be made good

and provision made for the children of the first marriage. If the children have unjustly been alienated and removed from the innocent divorced or deserted spouse they should be restored to this parent, to the extent that this is humanly possible and is the best thing for the children themselves.

(3) The unfaithful spouse who has given offence must make it clear over a certain period of time that he or she honestly wishes to return to the practice of the faith.

If all these essential conditions are fulfilled as far as possible, then the path of sacramental reconciliation must also be open, even if it is humanly impossible to give up the second marriage that began in sin. One must also help the penitent to make a personal decision in conscience. A psychotherapeutic approach is also needed in his or her case. My opinion is that, given all these conditions, a solution in the internal forum can and should exist in individual cases – but not as a routine. But despite all the change of consciousness within the Church very great caution is needed in these cases even today before one can think of admitting such people to the sacraments in a parish in which memory of the offence is still very much alive. I have heard myself from innocent divorced and deserted spouses and from their relatives of how shocked they were to see the destroyer of a previous sound marriage approach the sacraments. Profound emotions should not be wounded in this way. If a human reconciliation has taken place or at least a serious effort made to bring this about, then admission to the sacraments in the person's own parish should rather be possible.

The practice and discipline of the early Church in East and West energetically combatted behaviour that was destructive of marriage, and those who were guilty and had given grave offence were subjected to severe penitential discipline. But very early on there was an arduous struggle over the amount of penance that could be expected and the length of time it should last. In this a clear distinction was drawn between serious sins on the one hand and on the other sins that gave serious offence. This seems to me to be important today in connection with the grey zone between a more or less innocent separation and divorce and remarriage that give rise to serious offence. But in every case the Church's healing mission takes precedence over its judicial function.

In making moral judgements and with regard to the extent of the penance to be demanded a distinction is to be drawn over whether the second marriage (or cohabitation in a manner similar to marriage) has taken place with the accomplice in the sins that broke the marriage up or with someone who had nothing to do with this offence. The harshness of penitential discipline should not affect the innocent too, to the extent that this can be avoided. The kind of penitential discipline must in all cases point to the All-merciful and his healing love. But what must be demanded unconditionally is a profound conversion, turning away from evil, and turning humbly and gratefully to God.

In conclusion

Since we have all been redeemed by Christ and are in need of forgiveness, we are linked to other sinners at a profound level in a community of solidarity.

If we are harsh with regard to others and look on them with contempt, we link ourselves into the unredeemed and unsaved community of the self-righteous. If, on the contrary, we live in gratitude in and from the community of salvation, thanks to unmerited grace, then for us there are no "hopeless cases".

As a holy penitent the Church should make visible to all not only the demanding seriousness of following Christ in discipleship but even more the healing love of the Redeemer that seeks people out.

The Church as a whole and every individual Christian should become a perceptible sign of God's saving and liberating grace.

In a profoundly experienced solidarity of salvation we wish to strive together, in gratitude for grace and in awareness of our weakness, for the true freedom and faithfulness to which Christ has called us. To this belongs also being free and continually becoming free from unsuitable harshness and loveless judgement.

It is only in amazement at the unmerited reconciliation and healing which is continually being brought about in us afresh and in continuous praise of the all-merciful divine Father that we are healed of our blindness, freed from all self-righteousness, and thus enabled to become credible signs of the faithful, healing love of the Good Shepherd. For this we need not least the gift of discernment of spirits, which the "Spirit of Truth", the "Comforter", promised us by Christ wishes to bestow on us.

Notes

[1] Eloquent evidence for this is provided by the article by Otto F. ter Reegen, officialis of the archdiocese of Utrecht, "Geschiedene in der Kälte stehen lassen?", in *Diakonia* 19 (1988), pp. 334-340.

[2] In this context one should read a statement by the head of the John Paul II Institute, Mgr Carlo Caffarra, an influential adviser of the Pope on questions of marriage, who told a congress of moral theologians he himself organized in November 1988: "That is why the man who has raised himself to the ethical level no longer concerns himself at all or ultimately with the possibilities, consequences, or historical outcomes of his action: he is placed above such calculation" ("Humanae vitae: 20 anni dopo". *Atti del II Congresso Internazionale di Teologia Morale*, Roma 9-12 novembre 1988, p. 188). This would seem to exclude a teleologically-oriented ethic of responsibility. This is something that needs determined opposition in the name of sound Catholic moral theology.

[3] *Theologia moralis*, VI §900 cf §882; see B. Häring, *Free and Faithful in Christ* II, p. 521, Slough 1979.

[4] J. Ratzinger/H.D. Wendland, *Theologie der Ehe*, 83f., Regensburg [2]1972.

[5] *Sermo*, 74:2; *PL* 54:398.

[6] *Ennaratio in Psalmum* 103; *PL* 37:1348.

[7] The justification mentioned here for excluding remarried divorcees – even in the case when one has to admit that responsibility forbids them to separate – is dominant in the apostolic exhortation *Familiaris consortio*. On the question of what it really means "objectively" to be living in a state of grave sin one could read many an over-rigorous churchman a long penitential sermon, for example with regard to clerical vanity, honorary titles and transport. Does not a state of grave sin exist "objectively" in this case too from time to time? And in such a case must not someone remain excluded from the sacraments until he has relinquished his position and his titles?

[8] With regard to this I refer especially to Urs Baumann, *Die Ehe – ein Sakrament?*, Zürich 1988, with its three instructive and informative sections (*Die kirchliche Lehre*, pp. 23-139, *Fundamente*, pp. 141-268, and *Ansätze und Lösungen in der Theologie der Gegenwart*, pp. 269-377). The book also contains a comprehensive bibliography on the subjects we are interested in here (pp. 465-501), apart from the numerous valuable references to sources

in the notes (pp. 395-501). Concise treatment of these questions is to be found in the special issue of *Diakonia* on marriage and patterns of living together outside marriage, cf. especially the contributions of Alois Müller, "Für eine Neuorientierung der katholischen Ehelehre" in *Diakonia* 19 (1988), pp. 301-305, and Walter Kirchschläger, "Ehe und Ehescheidung – Rückfragen an Bibel und Kirche", *ibid.*, pp. 305-316.

[9] The texts are to be found in Isabel Florence Hapgood, *Service Book of the Holy Orthodox-Catholic Apostolic Church*, pp. 304-305, Brooklyn, NY 1965.

[10] *Theologia moralis* I, §201; cf. B. Häring, *Free and Faithful in Christ* I, p. 363, Slough ³1985.

[11] *Ibid.* VI, §947.

[12] This possibility is indicated among others by Barry Brunsman, *New Hope for Divorced Catholics: A Concerned Pastor Offers Alternatives to Annulment*, San Francisco 1985, and by the ever-cautious Professor Karl Hörmann, *Kirche und die zweite Ehe*, Innsbruck 1973. On 5 May 1973, the Austrian Bishops' Theological Commission, which studied this question on behalf of the Austrian Bishops' Conference, "noted with agreement" Professor Hörmann's study (p. 9).

[13] In the section that follows I repeat, in different words, what I expounded in 1969 in a document requested for an English-speaking association of canon lawyers. After this had been thoroughly debated both in England and in North America I gave permission for it to be published under the title "Internal Forum Solutions to Insoluble Marriage Cases" in *The Jurist* 30 (1970), pp. 21-30. The article was soon published in German translation in Hans Heimerl (ed.), *Verheiratet und doch nicht verheiratet?* pp. 141-153, Vienna 1970, under the title "Lösungen im Gewissensbereich für unlösbare Ehefälle". I would like to point out that the translation *im Gewissensbereich* ("in the field of conscience") is imprecise, since I was concerned with solutions that could include sacramental absolution. I have made this position of mine known in numerous other publications in several languages. It has received much approval but also disapproval, though it has not attracted any reprimand from Church officialdom.

[14] Quoted from Barry Brunsman, *op. cit.*, pp. 79-80.

St Paul Publications

Books by Bernard Häring

Free and faithful in Christ

Moral theology for priests and laity

Radiating hope, Christian joy and vision
on every page, Fr Häring has provided
us with an up-to-date work of beauty,
simplicity and vision. Written out of his
own experience of the ways of the Spirit,
he keeps the reader's mind fixed
throughout on the power of Christ
and the liberating action of the Spirit.
In three volumes:

    I – General moral theology
    II – The truth will make you free
    III – Light to the world/Salt for the earth

each volume £12.00

Manipulation

*Ethical boundaries of medical,
behavioural and genetic manipulation*

The problems approached in this work
are the concern not only of moralists,
members of the medical profession,
scientists and legislators, but of all
mature people who wish to participate
in the process of making decisions.
The areas covered include those of
education, public opinion, biology,
psychological therapy, psycho-surgery
and genetics.

paperback £6.50   hardback £7.95

Bernard Häring

The Sacred Heart of Jesus and the redemption of the world

The devotion to the Sacred Heart of our Redeemer, as proposed by the teaching and the liturgy of the Church, is "the cult of love... the synthesis of the mystery of our religion". These thirty meditations are based on holy Scripture, tradition, the liturgy and the teaching of the Church.

£4.95

Timely and untimely virtues

Virtues are something very beautiful, grace-filled, always timely, of abiding value. What do we mean by virtue? Which virtues should we aim at? Fr Häring's reflection centres on timely virtues: timely in the sense that our present times need urgently these virtues, not only urgently but that they would be the greatest asset to present history. He elaborates on the biblical virtues which aim to make us creative participants into the history of salvation.

£2.95

 St Paul Publications

Bernard Häring

**The healing
power of peace
and
non-violence**

A new approach: a therapeutic
spirituality and strategy. Many
theological and pastoral concerns
flow together in this treatise.
The fundamental elements is a
coherent, therapeutic understanding
of redemption, reconciliation and
liberation, as found in the best
Christian tradition. This is one of
Fr Häring's major studies: it works out
a dimension of the peace-problem
so far scarcely touched.

£4.95

**Prayer:
the integration
of faith and life**

"A person who has found his integration
in prayer can do more for the evangeli-
sation of today than can hundreds of
restless activists..." In these rewarding
meditations, Fr Häring gives us a large
number of short passages in which there
are many sound observations about
prayer – which lead into prayers of his
own.

£3.95

 St Paul Publications

Bernard Häring

Medical ethics

A careful and conscious study of the main issues in medical ethics today: life, death, contraception, abortion, artificial insemination, sterilisation, prolongation of life, euthanasia, drugs, psychotherapy, experimentation with human beings... This is an impressive work of scholarship – very topical and readable – a book that deserves to be read by doctors, nurses, priests, and indeed by all mature reflecting Christians and others.

£6.95

The sacrament of reconciliation

Through a series of scripture passages the author leads the reader – penitent or confessor – into an understanding of reconciliation that reaches beyond the mere recital of faults: not ritualism, but a communal celebration of sorrow in which the penitent recognises his need of forgiveness – a need that overflows into thankfulness to the Lord who had already forgiven all through his redeeming death.

£2.95

 St Paul Publications

Bernard Häring

The Eucharist and our everyday life

Fr Häring wrote this little book as an act of thanksgiving for the gift of faith and the priestly vocation.
It is offered as an invitation to make the Eucharistic thanksgiving and praise – the Mass – the leitmotif and norm for our everyday life, thus bringing home all of our life into the Eucharist.

£2.95

Healing and revealing

The author reflects on the need for an organic synthesis of the message of salvation and the healing ministry to sick people as well as sick cultures and societies.
He looks at the main causes and symptoms afflicting humankind today, and focuses his attention on the Church's mission and actual *diakonia* of healing.

£4.50

 St Paul Publications

Bernard Häring

**Called
to holiness**

'How can I become holy?'
The vocation to holiness is the central
message of the Bible.
In a series of eleven meditations
Fr Häring leads the reader through
appropriate Scripture texts to an
understanding of what holiness
entails, the pitfalls that await the
unwary, the link between suffering
and holiness, and the overall goal
of seeking perseverance to the end.

£2.95

Holiness in today's world

**Christian
maturity**

Holiness is an obligation that flows
from one's baptismal commitment.
It is not something that can be
privatised: it must go public.
The ramifications of its doing so
mean that while faithfulness to the
gospel guarantees Christian identity
that very fidelity exacts of every
Christian a continual growth in
maturity. In this book Bernard Häring
outlines the social implications of
being a Christian in today's world.

£4.95

 St Paul Publications